Missionary Anecdotes.—Frontispiece.

Chinese Praying Machine.

MISSIONARY ANECDOTES.

SERIES FIRST.

THE ISLANDS OF THE PACIFIC;
INDIA AND BURMAH; CHINA; NORTH AFRICA AND TURKEY;
SOUTH AFRICA AND MADAGASCAR; NORTH AMERICA
AND THE WEST INDIES.

WITH TWELVE ILLUSTRATIONS.

PHILADELPHIA:
AMERICAN SUNDAY-SCHOOL UNION,
No. 1122 Chestnut Street.

NEW YORK:
Nos. 8 & 10 Bible House, Astor Place.

Reprinted from the London Edition, after revision by the Committee of Publication.

PREFACE.

AMIDST the multitude of works of a missionary character that now abound, the want has been felt of a concise collection of some of the more striking facts for the use of any whose reading of this kind is limited, or of those who are trying to interest others in the subject; and the following pages are simply an attempt to supply this want.

In our days it would be, happily, no difficult matter to collect many such facts as would serve abundantly to illustrate the working of the grace of God in the various heathen countries to which his word has recently been carried. The only difficulty is in making a selection. Ill, indeed, has the Church obeyed her Saviour's parting charge; but now that in these latter days she has somewhat awakened to a sense of her heavy responsibility in this matter, his blessing has so abundantly rested on the feeble efforts made, that results have followed far beyond what the originators of our various societies could possibly have anticipated in so short a space of time. To bring out some of these results has been the aim of the compiler of the present little volume, the contents of which have, of course, been drawn from many sources. Some anecdotes have been taken from the memoirs of departed missionaries; many from the various periodicals of the different societies; while for some interesting matter, the writer is indebted to the narratives of Williams and Moffat, to the London Missionary Society's work on Madagascar, to that of the Bishop of Waiapu on New Zealand, to the Rev. J. Baillie's "Rivers in the Desert," to Mrs. Ellis's "Trials and Triumphs," to Miss Tucker's "Rainbow in the North," to Miss Whately's "Ragged Life in Egypt," to the Rev. E. B. Elliot's "Life of Lord Haddo," and to a work entitled "Perils among the Heathen."

Facts are the best answer to those who scoffingly ask, "What have missions effected?" They are the best of all encouragements to those whose hands are apt to hang down in despondency, because they convincingly prove that our God is faithful to his Word. And, next to the influence of that motive which must be the basis of all true missionary action, they are, perhaps, the most effectual means of stirring up an interest in the minds of those who have hitherto been lukewarm, or even cold.

It is, therefore, in the earnest hope that some little help may thereby be rendered towards the great work of the Church during the absence of her Lord, that this small collection of anecdotes is offered to the Christian world.

MISSIONARY FACTS AND ANECDOTES.

THE ISLANDS OF THE PACIFIC.

John Williams and his Work.—Raratonga gives up its Idols.—Old Me, the Blind Warrior of Raiatea.—The first Sabbath kept in New Zealand.—The Trials of the Missionaries.—Education for the Priesthood.—Tamahana te Rauparaha; or, seeking after Truth.—Tamahana goes to seek a Teacher—The Peacemaker.—Fiji and its People.—John Hunt and his Fellow-Labourers—Visit to a Fijian Island.

WHEN, in the end of the last century, a missionary spirit began to revive in the Church, the London Missionary Society, which was one of the first founded, and which then comprehended both Churchmen and Dissenters, began its labours on a large scale among the islands of the Pacific Ocean. They purchased a ship, and sent out twenty-five labourers to commence missions simultaneously at the Marquesan, Tahitian, and Friendly Isles. They went out bearing precious seed, and no doubt hoping soon to see it take root and bring forth much fruit.

But though "God's promises all are true, they are not dated;" we must ever bide his time. And so it was in this case. A night of weeping had to be passed through before the morning of joy came.

The Marquesan mission at that time failed; at the Friendly Isles some of the missionaries lost their lives; while the ship "Duff" was, on its second voyage out, captured by a French privateer, all the property lost, and the new missionaries which it carried compelled to return to England. Some of the first party, however, remained at their posts, while others returned after a time; and at Tahiti some devoted men laboured on patiently for many years without a single convert; until, at length, such terrible wars raged among the natives, that for a while they were obliged to quit the island. It was during their absence that the work began in the following way:—

Two native servants who, unknown to their teachers, had received spiritual impressions, began to unite in prayer. Others soon joined them; so that when the missionaries returned, they found a great number of "pure atua," or praying people; and ere long even the king placed himself under instruction, and sought for baptism.

Meantime the directors at home, knowing nothing of this (for communication with distant lands was slow in those days), were consulting on the advisability of abandoning a mission on which fifteen years of fruitless toil had been expended. A few only opposed the measure; but their words and renewed contributions prevailed; and, instead of the order to withdraw, letters of encouragement were forwarded to the missionaries.

Strange to say, the very ship which carried these letters was crossed by another vessel conveying to England not only the news of the entire overthrow of idolatry, but also the rejected idols of the people.

This news reached England in October, 1813.

Extract of a Letter from King Pomare at Tahiti, dated February 17, 1813, to the Missionaries at Eimeo.

"MY DEAR FRIENDS.—May Jehovah and Jesus Christ bless you, and me also, this evil man, whose crimes are accumulated. I perfectly agree to your request in your letter lately wrote to me, my dear friends, in which you desire my permission to cut down the Tamanu* and the Amai. Cut them down without regarding consequences, for a keel to our vessel. What will

* Probably sacred trees.

be the consequence? Shall we be destroyed by the evil spirits? We cannot be destroyed by them; we have a great Saviour, Jesus Christ. Where you lead, regardless of consequences, I, this evil man, will follow.

"The Three-One can (or will) make me good. I venture with my guilt (or evil deeds) to Jesus Christ, though I am not equalled in wickedness, not equalled in guilt, not equalled in obstinate disobedience and rejection of the truth, that this very wicked man may be saved by Jehovah and Jesus Christ. . . .

"May the Three-One bless you and us also. May we all be saved by Jesus Christ, our only (or true) Saviour. POMARE."

JOHN WILLIAMS AND HIS WORK.

In 1817, the celebrated John Williams, now known as the martyr of Erromanga, entered on his missionary labours at the chief of the Society Isles, Raiatea; but he soon longed to carry the Gospel "to the regions beyond;" and in order to reach the Hervey and Navigator's Islands, he actually himself constructed a vessel, after having first made the tools with which to work. This done, his plan was to leave native converts in the various islands, to tell to others the good news which they themselves had learned. These he himself superintended and visited, and in his own words, after referring to the long waiting time which his predecessors had passed through at Tahiti and other places, we have the result given.

"From that time to this," he says, "one continued series of successes has attended our labours, so that island after island, and group after group, have, in rapid succession, been brought under the influence of the Gospel; so much so, indeed, that at the present time we do not know of any group, or any single island of importance, within two thousand miles of Tahiti, in any direction, to which the glad tidings of salvation have not been conveyed."

RARATONGA GIVES UP ITS IDOLS.

This was an island which had escaped the researches of Captain Cook, but having heard of it from the natives of some of the other islands, Mr. Williams determined, if possible, to find it. At Aitutaki he found six Raratongans, who had there embraced Christianity; and these he carried back to their own land, with some teachers from Raiatea and their wives.

It was some time before the island could be found; and this being the first visit paid to its inhabitants by Europeans, they doubted as to their favourable reception. A hearty welcome, however, awaited them. The Raratongans were not only glad to see their own countrymen back; —they had been prepared for the strangers, also, by a woman who had been conveyed thither from Tahiti. She had told the Raratongans that they were not the only people in the world, but that there were also white people called Cookees,* who had introduced wonderful improvements into Tahiti; so that they no longer used stone axes and hatchets, nor human bones for tools, nor shark's teeth to cut the children's hair, nor were they obliged to go down to the water to look at themselves. Though a heathen still herself, she had also told enough about the Christian religion to make the Raratongans wish to know more of it; so the king himself went off to the vessels to receive the teachers, and conduct them to the shore.

The chiefs and people joined in the welcome. They desired them to remain, and said that it would be good for them to teach the Word of God; but as they also insisted that it would be good for the chiefs to have the teachers' wives, the party were obliged to return to the ship,

---

* All Europeans were so called by these islanders after Captain Cook.

and with much regret this field of labour was about to be abandoned, when Papeiha, a most devoted native evangelist, who had already done good service at Aitutaki, offered to remain alone.

Feeling that his property would not be safe among such utterly barbarous people, he returned to the island with nothing but the clothes that he wore, his native Testament, and a bundle of elementary books; but happily he was not quite without friends, for the little company of converted Raratongans who had returned to their island in the vessel were warmly attached to him, and they promised to remain steadfast.

Four months after this a colleague was sent to support him; and by that time many had joined the little band. When rather more than a year had elapsed from the discovery of the island, two gentlemen, Messrs. Tyerman and Bennet, who had been sent from England to inspect all these missions, paid Raratonga a visit, and found that the whole population had renounced idolatry, and were engaged in building a large chapel.

Whilst this work was going on, Mr. and Mrs. Williams came to stay for some time among the people. They found the teachers established in very comfortable houses, one of which was immediately given up for their use; and a day or two after their arrival they were requested to take their seats outside the doors. No sooner had they done so, than a large crowd of people appeared approaching them with heavy burdens. They came in procession, and dropped at their feet fourteen immense idols, the smallest of which was about five yards long. Most of these were instantly destroyed before their faces; others were reserved to decorate the roof of the chapel, and one was afterwards sent home to be placed in the missionary museum.

OLD ME, THE BLIND WARRIOR OF RAIATEA.

In the island of Raiatea there once lived a warrior who was the terror of that and many other islands. In the last battle fought before the introduction of Christianity, he received a blow which deprived him of sight, and not long after the lion was changed into a lamb; for he was one of the first members of the Raiatean church. He used to attend the adult schools diligently, in order by listening to learn all he could, and was constantly to be seen at the chapel, whither he was led by one kind friend or another, he holding one end of a stick, and his guide the other, the guide sometimes being a chief, or even the king himself.

On his return from Raratonga, Mr. Williams missed old Me from his place in the house of God, and, on inquiring, found that he was ill and not likely to recover. "Do I really hear your voice again? I shall die happy now," was the old man's welcome on his first visit. And then the missionary proceeded to inquire how he was cared for and supplied with food; for even the best of the people had not yet so thoroughly outgrown their old habits of barbarity towards the sick as to be always quite careful in this matter. In this case it turned out that there had been much cruel neglect, and yet Me had never complained, lest the people should call him a tale-bearer, and speak evil of his religion. He was then asked what Christian brethren had visited him in his affliction. Naming several, he added: "They do not come so often as I could wish; yet I am never lonely, for I have frequent visits from God; God and I were talking when you came in."

"Well, and what were you talking about?" asked Mr. Williams.

"I was praying to depart and be with Christ, which is far better," he replied.

He was then asked what he thought of himself in the sight of God, and what was the foundation of his hope.

"Ah," he said, "I have been in great trouble this morning, but I am happy now. I saw an immense mountain, with precipitous sides, up which I endeavoured to climb; but when I had attained a considerable height, I lost my hold and fell to the bottom. Exhausted with perplexity and fatigue, I went to a distance and sat down to weep, and while weeping, I saw a drop of blood fall upon that mountain, and in a moment it was dissolved."

"This was a strange sight," said his pastor; "what construction do you put upon it?"

He was surprised at the question, and exclaimed, "That mountain was my sins, and the drop which fell upon it was one drop of the precious blood of Jesus, by which the mountain of my guilt must be melted away."

Mr. Williams soon after said that he would go home and prepare some medicine for him, on which he said, "I shall drink it because you say I must, but I shall not pray to be restored to health again, for my desire is to depart and be with Christ, which is far better than to remain in this sinful world."

It was not long ere he had his wish. He expired crying, "O death, where is thy sting?"

THE FIRST SABBATH KEPT IN NEW ZEALAND.

It was in 1814, and within a few days of the close of that year, that the Rev. Samuel Marsden, chaplain of the convict settlement of Paramatta, near Sydney, accompanied the first missionaries and their families to New Zealand. Six years before he had met with some of the natives of those isles in the streets of Paramatta, and been struck with their noble appearance and intellectual superiority. Then that idea entered his mind which afterwards took such possession of it as to influence all his future life, and to procure for him the title of "the apostle of New Zealand." He determined that, with God's help, the New Zealanders should have the gospel. During a visit to England he laid the matter before the Church Missionary Committee, who fully approved the design, and for years seemed to look to him as the father and superintendent of the work.

But these islanders were known to be warlike and ferocious cannibals; and, moreover, the conduct of Europeans in their dealings with them had not been such as to produce any friendly feelings towards the English; so, though these missionaries had come out in 1809, yet events occurred which obliged them to wait in New

South Wales until it should seem safe for them to proceed.

During the interval Mr. Marsden endeavored to cultivate friendly relations with the people, of whom there were generally a few in the colony; and he sometimes had as many as thirty of these visitors in the parsonage at Paramatta. Among them were the chiefs Ruatara and George, both of whom had suffered insults and injuries on board English vessels in which they had made voyages, but by intercourse with him had learned that all the English were neither cruel nor perfidious. These, by their influence, had prepared the way for him, and it was off Rangihoua, Ruatara's own village, that the missionary ship cast anchor.

Some influential chiefs came forward to welcome their visitors, and to promise them support and protection. The next day was Sunday, and of his own accord Ruatara set to work to make preparations for a service. He enclosed about half an acre of ground, set up a pulpit and reading-desk in the centre, which he covered with cloth brought from Port Jackson, and lastly arranged some canoes as seats.

Next morning, Mr. Marsden saw the English flag flying from a flag-staff erected by Ruatara, and about one o'clock nearly the whole of the ship's crew accompanied him on shore. Ruatara and two other chiefs met him, dressed in regimentals which had been given them, each also wearing a sword and having a switch in his hand. Their men were drawn up on each side; and when the English were seated, the inhabitants of the town, including the women and children, formed a circle round them.

"I rose up," says Mr. Marsden, "and began the service by singing the Hundredth Psalm, and felt my very soul melt within me when I viewed my congregation, and considered the state they were in. After reading the service, during which the natives stood up and sat down at the signal given by the motion of Korokoro's switch, which was regulated by the movements of the Europeans. It being Christmas day, I preached from the second chapter of Luke, and the tenth verse, 'Behold, I bring you glad tidings of great joy.' The natives told Ruatara that they could not understand what I said. He replied that they were not to mind that now; for they would understand by and by; and that he would explain my meaning as far as he could. When I had done preaching, he informed them what I had been talking about. In this manner has the gospel been introduced into New Zealand."

Notwithstanding this prosperous beginning, the labourers had to wait ten years even for the first fruits; yet Mr. Marsden lived to see many of these poor savages enlisted under the banner of his Master; and, at his seventh and last visit to the island, he met large companies of Christians in various stations, and was greeted by all, whether heathen or Christians, as a father and a friend.

DAILY TRIALS OF THE MISSIONARIES.

Many were the trials which the missionaries had to bear before any token of success was granted to cheer their hearts; but the worst of these did not come on them during the life-time of those friendly chiefs who had first received and protected them. It was in the year 1821 that one of them wrote: "This morning (Sunday) many natives rushed in to Mr. Puckey's yard and others into his kitchen, using abusive language, and seizing whatever they pleased. We were all in consternation, not knowing to what length they might go. Mr. Puckey with his wife and children were crying and entreating; and as for me, my place being next, I expected them to break in every moment. However, Rewa, who has always been our friend, came running down, and turned them all out; but they car-

Missionaries Plundered by New Zealanders. p. 21.

ried off many articles. Mr. Puckey's son was sleeping in the kitchen; and when they broke in, two of them laid hold of him by the hair, and held a hatchet over him, threatening to cut off his head if he spoke a word. At length peace was restored; but my mind was so much agitated that it was with difficulty I got through the morning service. We had scarcely begun when Mr. Puckey was called out; for the natives were taking his chickens. He went and begged them to desist, but they took them all away. The same day they broke into poor Mr. Puckey's house again, when the dinner was on the table, and took away all the food, besides breaking the plates and dishes, and stealing the knives and forks."

EDUCATION FOR THE PRIESTHOOD.

The New Zealanders had no settled form of religion, nor deities to whom regular worship was paid; nevertheless, there were priests whose services were required at special times, such as war or sickness, and these priests were supposed to have the power of bewitching whom they pleased. Their training for the office was a simple drawing out of every evil disposition. "Before I was born," says one, who became a convert to Christianity, "my father devoted me to the powers of darkness. As soon as I was able to struggle for my mother's breast, I was often teased by my father, and kept from it in order that angry passions might be deeply rooted in me. The stronger I grew, the more I was teased by my father, and the harder I had to fight for nourishment. All this was done before I was old enough to notice the plants which are produced by the earth. When I could run about, the work of preparation went on more rigidly; and my father kept me without food that I might learn to thieve, not forgetting, at the same time, to stir up the spirit of anger and revenge which he had so assiduously endeavoured to plant in my breast. My father then taught me how to bewitch and destroy at my pleasure; and he told me that to be a great man I must be a bold murderer, a desperate and expert thief, and able to do all kinds of wickedness effectually."

TAMAHANA TE RAUPARAHA; OR, SEEKING AFTER TRUTH.

Tamahana Te Rauparaha was a young New Zealand chief, whose father, grandfather, and great grandfathers seem to have been men of renown among the warriors of their nation. Tamahana was brought up in a part of the country that was five hundred miles distant from any mission station; and his early youth was spent amidst scenes of bloodshed, for Te Rauparaha, his father, was always engaged in making conquests, and constantly at war with one or another of the neighbouring chiefs.

Tamahana was born after a great fight; and the same day his mother tried to kill him. That was not an unusual thing in those dark days; but this baby was to live to do a great work among his people. So the father heard the infant's cry, and rushed in before the poor mother's cruel purpose was accomplished. He put him in a basket and carried him away, and while still very little, the child was taken by him to the priest to be blessed, who prayed that he might grow up "strong to fight, be brave, and fear nothing."

That prayer was heard by One mightier than any being of whom this poor heathen chief had ever heard; and the boy, whom he had named "the white chief bird of heaven," soon began to show himself strong, brave, and fearless, only not in the way in which the father desired.

As a little boy, he tells us, he did not believe in the gods of his fathers. He saw that they were no gods, though at that time he had heard of no better way. So, when his father used to hang up food in a tree for the gods, and the priests said that they ate some, and that the rest was for them, he went to his father and asked, "Why should the priest eat all? Why should they not give me some?" The father said that the food was "tapu," that is, "holy;" but Tamahana ventured, and when his father was gone, he crept along the ground, took the food and eat it. Te Rauparaha was angry when he found this out, and said that the god would kill his son; but the boy said, "I do not fear; I am safe." The god did not kill him; and less than ever did he believe in the gods of his fathers.

He was a wild boy then, and a bad one too, by his own confession; but he could not be happy without any god at all; and very plainly we can see from the story, in which he tells about himself, that God was preparing his heart to receive the good seed.

It was sown there before many years had passed, in a very wonderful way.

There was a youth named Matahau, belonging to the same tribe as that to which Tamahana's mother had belonged, who had been carried as a prisoner to the Bay of Islands. There he had met with Christian missionaries, and in one of their schools he had learned to read. After awhile Matahau came back with a number of his tribe to visit his old friends at Otaki, and Tamahana heard that they had seen white men who had told them about the great God in the heavens; that they had a book given them by these white men, and that three of them could read this book. His "heart wished," he says, "to hear more of that Word;" so he went to Matahau and said, "Where is the book?" But Matahau only said, "Another man has it; you go and take it."

To this other man, therefore, Tamahana and his cousin, Te Whiwhi, went, eager to gain possession of the treasure; but he said, "No, I cannot give it you; I want it for cartridges."

"Oh! you give it," said Tamahana. "It is the book of God. You must not use it for your gun." And by dint of persuasion, and a present of mats and tobacco, they at last got the book.

It was of no use, however, until they could read it; so Tamahana, Te Whiwhi, and ten of their companions, asked Matahau to teach them. But Matahau had no love for the Word of God himself, and did not seem to like the trouble of teaching it; so he said, "Do not read that book; it is a bad book; it tells not to have two wives, not to drink rum, not to fight, but to live in peace, and to pray to God." And the people with him spoke in the same way. Tamahana shall tell the rest of the story.

"I said to Te Whiwhi, 'Never mind their words, let us read.' My heart and Te Whiwhi's, and the other young men's, longed to hear the new talk. Because I did not believe in the old way, that was why I wanted to learn the new way. Matahau read the Catechism first to us,—the young men and children. The old men did not like the new talk; they liked the fight.

"When Matahau had finished reading the Catechism, I spoke out loud to the ten young men. I said, 'Those words are good words; I believe all.' Te Whiwhi said so too, and Uremutu, another cousin, also said, 'I believe it is true talk; the talk of the book. If there were no book, only the talk of Matahau, we would not believe; but the book talks true.' Te Whiwhi said, 'If you do not believe, I do.' And he and I said we would take Matahau to Kapiti to teach us, that we might be quiet. He did not like to come; but I talked to him, and pulled him, and he came. Te Whiwhi and I were kind to him; we gave him food and clothes, and every thing. After we had gone to Kapiti, my uncle Watanui came to us to tell us to come to the fight at Waitotara. But I said, 'No, I will not go to fight. I fear the book of God. I believe it. I will not go.' Te Whiwhi said so too. Before, Te Whiwhi had been very strong in fight. He did not fear the sword. He had killed many men. My uncle and father were very angry with us. They said, 'Our gods are the true gods. They have made us strong to kill so many people. Your God is not strong.' But we would not go.

"We were at Kapiti with Matahau near six months. We learnt every day, every night. We did not lie down to sleep. We sat at night in the hut, all around the fire in the middle. Te Whiwhi had part of the book and I part. Sometimes we went to sleep upon the book for a little while, then woke up and read again. After we had been there six months we could read a little, very slowly. Then we went across in a canoe to Waikanne. We brought Matahau to teach the Ngatiawa people about the book. Those people liked it very much; they believed. Then they all wanted the book. I told them I could not give them my part of Luke; but I told Matahau to write for them on paper, 'Our Father,' etc. Matahau wrote for them all, and then they all learnt. He wrote also the letter for them, and taught them to read. Before, Matahau had not believed, but now his heart began to grow. We talked to him, and he believed."

TAMAHANA GOES TO SEEK A TEACHER.

Tamahana and his cousin were very uncommon young men. Christian England has few such noble characters. Having found the truth themselves, they were determined, at all hazards, to find some one who could teach it to their people. Besides, they did not fully trust to Matahau, and longed to hear the words straight from a white man's mouth.

An American ship came to their shores on its way to the Bay of Islands. So direct to his father went Tamahana, declaring that he and Te Whiwhi would go and fetch a missionary. Te Rauparaha was angry, and so were all the chiefs. They did not want a missionary among them, and said if Tamahana went to the Bay of Islands he would be killed; but the young man replied, "Never mind if they kill me; I want to kill your bad ways."

The father went to the captain of the ship to tell him not to take his son; but Tamahana, when he heard it, said, "You must take us, for we have paid you." They had paid for their passage many pigs and potatoes. Tamahana was only seventeen or eighteen at this time;

but he had been married two years. His wife cried, and tore her clothes when he left her; and he said, "I was sorry for my wife, but happy to go. After I was gone, my father did not eat for three days. He feared I should be killed. He feared also that the Gospel should come." The youth knew of the sorrow of both father and wife, but he knew also that "he that loveth father or mother, wife or children," more than Jesus Christ, is not worthy of him. He knew him to be the pearl of great price for whom the whole world must be given up. Besides, he was thoroughly bent on bringing the knowledge of this priceless pearl within the reach of all whom he loved.

When they came to the Bay of Islands, a little fear came over him; but he said to his cousin, "Never mind; God will take care of us."

The first chief whom he met was Pomare, who had married his cousin. He received them in a friendly way, but was much surprised to find that they were "missionary men," and that they wanted Archdeacon Williams, whom they called Te Wiremu Karuwa, or four eyes, because he wore spectacles.

Pomare said: "Ah! the missionaries are very bad. They do not drink or fight; they do not like the whaling-men, who give us muskets, grog, and any thing."

But the young men were not turned from their purpose. From the very first, they had met with difficulties and discouragements; but their minds were made up; and the next day they found out the missionary.

He asked, "Why have you come?" but when they told him, he could only say, "There is no missionary that we can send."

"Then," says Tamahana, "I was very sorry. I talked, talked; oh! how many hours I talked. Another day we came again and talked."

Mr. Williams said, "Do you know the potatoes? When they are put in the ground they do not come up at once; after two or three weeks they come up."

He said, "Friend, we know potatoes do not grow fast on bad ground; but in the good ground, the warm ground, they come up quick." Then he laughed, and they went back to their ship.

But after a week they returned to the charge; and then Mr. Williams, unable to help them himself, sent them on to his brother. It was a distance of fifteen miles, and they travelled in constant fear of their enemies, the Ngapui, and on their arrival, another disappointment awaited them; for, like his brother, Mr. W. Williams was obliged to say, "We cannot send a missionary, for we have not one to spare."

"Oh! my heart was dark," says Tamahana; "there was a new missionary in the room. He was young and weak, not strong. He had just come to New Zealand, and could not understand Maori. I went back to Pahai. Oh! dark, very dark, our hearts were. We said, 'We have left our homes, our wives, and our people; we have come this long way, and now do not hear good talk.' I went to Te Wiremu Karuwa. I said, 'I am very sorry, very sorry. I do not like you; I cannot talk more to you. I shall go to my ship; I shall not come to you more. When I see you in my country, I shall not like you.' Then we went to our ship; very dark. We stayed in our cabin two weeks. The captain was painting the ship. That was why we stopped. One week more he would have finished it, and we should have gone back. One day, when we were at dinner, a sailor called out to us that 'the missionary's boat had come, and they are calling for you.' I left my dinner, and we ran quickly; for my heart was happy. We did not see the missionary, only we thought perhaps one had come for us. I went to the side of the ship, and spoke to Mr. Williams in the boat. Then he came to the ship. The young missionary whom we had seen before in his room was with him. His name was Mr. Hadfield. He had heard me speak to Mr. Williams that day; but he did not understand what we said. When we were gone, he said to Mr. Williams, 'What did those Maories say?' Mr. Williams told him that we wanted a missionary. Then God put it into his heart to like to come with us. When Mr. Williams came on the ship, he said, 'Friends, do not be angry with me more; here is your missionary.' We said, 'We are very much obliged to you;' and we were very happy. One week after, I started home in another ship, the 'Columbine,' with Mr. Hadfield, Mr. Williams, Mr. Clark, Mr. Stack, and Mr. Wilson, and also forty slaves, who were going back to their own places, and to preach the gospel."

At the end of six months from the time of Mr. Hadfield's arrival at Otaki, about twenty natives were baptized, and among them the young chiefs who had so zealously interested themselves in obtaining for their tribe the privileges and blessings of Christian instruction. Young Rauparaha then took the name of Tamahana, or Thompson, by which we have called him; Te Whiwhi was called Henera Matine—Henry Martyn; Uremuta had the name of Ha-

Hot Spring, or Geyser, in New Zealand. p. 33.

haraia—Zechariah; and Te Ahu that of Kiwai —Levi.

THE PEACEMAKER.

Archdeacon Henry Williams began his long course of forty-five years of labour in New Zealand in 1822, while wars were desolating the country, and before a single convert had gladdened the hearts of the missionaries. "He was not satisfied with preaching the Gospel to the natives, but at once attacked them on their own ground, following them to the field of battle; and thus he established an influence, unawares to themselves, which they were not prepared for. The efforts used were often successful; so that it became customary with the Ngapuhi chief to appeal at once to 'Te Wiremu.' The earliest of these cases occurred in the Bay of Islands, about 1827, immediately after which a favourable change took place; the natives acknowledged that the missionaries were right, and tribe after tribe expressed a desire to receive the Gospel." In later years since the differences between the natives and the colonists have rekindled a warlike spirit, the archdeacon thought it better not to interfere, because the government was established in the country; but on one occasion, when a battle was imminent, and many persons were trying to mediate a peace, Hone Heke, one of the chiefs, replied, with a sneer, "Who is going to listen to you? Where is our old father, Te Wiremu? Let him come and talk to us, and we will listen." He was accordingly sent for, and peace restored.

At the close of his life there was a serious quarrel about the ownership of a piece of land not far from Waimate. He was then too feeble to go among the natives as in old times; but his sons, on whom his mantle seems to have fallen, spent much time, day after day, in trying to effect a reconciliation.

The two parties had become exceedingly embittered against each other, and several lives having been lost, they were bent on obtaining satisfaction. On the day of the archdeacon's death, these young men, not believing their father in immediate danger, left home on their daily errand. A large number of the contending parties were gathered together; and they had come to the conclusion that next morning they would turn out into the open plain and fight it out. It seemed in vain to reason any longer with them; and a great slaughter was expected. But some time after dark the messenger came to announce to the sons that their father had passed away; and at once there arose the cry of lamentation from both camps. They had lost their common father, and, by a sudden impulse, both parties instantly agreed to a cessation of hostilities until the funeral was over. Soon after they decided to follow what they knew to be the dying wish of their benefactor, and make a general peace.

A great sifting-time has recently come on the New Zealand Church. During the late wars so many have fallen away, that some are ready to call the whole work a failure. But if many have gone back, many also remain steadfast, and adorn their profession; and at this present time there are thirteen native pastors supported by the contributions of their flocks.

FIJI AND ITS PEOPLE.

In the year 1835, two missionaries, with their wives and children, left Tonga, in the Friendly Isles, where they were beginning to reap the fruit of their labours, and proceeded to Lakemba, one of the Fiji group. The Tongans were good sailors, and had had frequent intercourse with the Fijians, whose language differed but little from their own; and the dreadful state of the latter people was therefore well known in the Friendly Isles. For even among savages the Fijians were counted savage; among cannibals they were reckoned vile; they had forgotten the common instincts of humanity, and stood unrivalled in brutality—a disgrace to mankind.

No wonder, then, that the Tongans, who had lately experienced a remarkable outpouring of the Holy Spirit, should desire to send among these, their wretched neighbours, that gospel whose transforming influence they had felt.

The missionaries themselves had long since determined to spend and be spent for Christ, and therefore the King of Tonga, having obtained a promise of protection for them from the King of Lakemba, they ventured even with their little ones.

At the end of the first year, seventy-nine adults and seventeen children were received into the church by baptism; at what a cost of labour, sickness, outraged feeling, and strong crying and tears, the missionary's God only knows. But those sufferings are over now, and theirs will be forever the rich reward.

JOHN HUNT AND HIS FELLOW-LABOURERS.

"Pity poor Fiji!" This was the cry which stirred the Methodist societies throughout England three years after the mission was commenced. It was sent home by the over-tasked labourers, and heard by John Hunt, among the other students of the Missionary College. But his destination to Africa had been already fixed; and when the directors sent for him, and asked if he would go to Fiji, the shock was great. "That poor girl in Lincolnshire!" he exclaimed to a fellow-student; "her mother will never consent." Yet feeling this request of the directors to be an intimation of the will of God, which he dared not disregard, he simply wrote to this young lady, to whom he had been ardently attached for six long years, begging her to get ready to accompany him in a month's time. She was by no means robust, and had been brought up in comfort; but her zeal was equal to his own, and the answer speedily came back that she "would go with him anywhere."

In January, 1839, the young couple reached their destination, and soon found that the half of Fiji's horrors had not been told them. But "I feel myself saved from almost all fear, though surrounded by men who have scarcely any regard for human life," were some of Mr. Hunt's first words home. "We are in the hands of a God whom even the heathen fear when they hear of him. The people at Lakemba say that their god has actually left the island, because our God has beaten him till his bones are sore."

Scarcely had the new missionaries gathered round them a little band of men and women, "whose hearts God had touched," than they were required to go and break up new ground in Somosomo, where even in Fiji the natives were counted vile; but they said, "We expect to sow in tears as confidently as we hope to reap in joy, and, therefore, trials and privations are words seldom used by us."

Mr. Lyth, a young brother missionary, accompanied them; and when the vessel reached Somosomo, a canoe, sent by the king, came off from the shore to receive them. It was half filled with naked cannibals; and as the ladies were lifted into it, men stood on the deck with loaded muskets and fixed bayonets to keep off the savages, among whom these ladies and their husbands were going to live.

About the time of their arrival, news came that one of the king's sons had been lost at sea; and, according to custom, it was forthwith ordered that all his wives should be strangled, that they might accompany him to the land of spirits. Here, then, was work for them; and the missionaries immediately went to the king to plead for the doomed women. Without success, however; and shortly after they heard the cries of the poor creatures and their friends; they were unmercifully strangled, and their bodies buried about twenty yards from the house.

It was not long before an epidemic influenza broke out, which the people chose to call the disease of the "lotu" (the word applied to those who turn Christians), and Mrs. Hunt was brought very low—first with this, and then with dysentery,—and while thus weakened her first child was born. The baby, too, soon became ill, and in a short time died. So, trial followed trial to the poor parents. The weather was too hot to allow of closed windows; and the natives had no idea of leaving them in peace. Once, when bending over her dying babe, Mrs. Hunt looked up to see dark, savage faces laughing and mocking at her anguish.

On another occasion a capricious chief who would be now their fast friend, now their enemy, flung open the Mission House, crying, "I am very angry;" and instantly seizing Mr. Hunt and Mr. Lyth, one in each hand, he drew them towards the door where he had left his club; but God preserved them. This same man, when in a gracious humour, would come and eat with them, regardless, sometimes, of their scanty stores. At times he would kneel down, and thrusting his face into that of the missionary, with strange grimaces and remarks, watch the stranger's way of eating, sweeping the plate as he did so with his ample beard.

It was hard work at Somosomo, because opposition was strong, and success long in coming. The king became irritated at their remonstrances against cannibalism; and they were often almost without food. "No," the king once said, in answer to their request, "I will not let you have food. Jehovah may give you a pig." "When it came to that," Mr. Hunt said, "I believe he will;" and shortly afterwards the king, being conciliated with a present, sent a pig as an offering to Jehovah.

At length threats were uttered against the missionaries' lives; the king and chiefs plainly told them that they were determined not to turn, and that they had better go. One night, there was every reason to believe that the murderous purpose of the savages was about to be carried into effect. A strange and gloomy night it was in that great gloomy house where the missionaries lived. The devoted men and women looked at each other and at their little ones, and felt as they only can feel who believe that their hours are numbered. Then they went all together for help to Him who ever shelters those who trust in him. Surrounded by native mosquito curtains, hung up to hide them from any who might be peeping through the frail reed walls of the house, this band of faithful ones, one after another, called upon God through the long hours of that terrible night, resolved that their murderers should find them at prayer. Just at midnight each pleading voice was hushed, and each head bowed lower as the stillness outside was suddenly broken by a loud and ringing shout. But the purpose of the people was changed; and that cry was but to call out the women to dance; and thus the night passed away.

An impression was being made even in Somosomo; and when Mr. Hunt was called on to go to Viva, he could say, "We believe that we have been made a blessing; though the fruits of our labours do not appear, and perhaps will not at present." After they had left, and when a time of great trouble had humbled the people, thousands forsook their idols, and turned to the Lord.

The good work begun at Viva, under Mr. Cross, prospered under Mr. Hunt's fostering care. There, in 1848, he finished his course, saying, "Let me go, a heap of inconsistencies, backslidings, and unfaithfulness. Let me go, as I trust I shall, through Divine mercy alone, —for I have nothing at all in myself—to heaven."

VISIT TO A FIJIAN ISLAND.

An interesting incident was lately related at Boston, by a sea captain belonging to that city. He said, that when in command of a ship in the Pacific, he had occasion to stop at one of the Fiji Islands, supposed to be inhabited by cannibals, and visited the shore in a boat, thoroughly armed, for fear of an attack by the natives, when, to his surprise, he was met and addressed in English by the chief of the island, who told him he and his people were all Christians, converted from their former wickedness by a missionary from the United States, and asked him to go to his hut and remain until next morning. He went; and at the close of the day, the Fijian told his guest that it was his custom, at the end of each day, to thank his heavenly Father for the day's blessings, and implore his protection for the ensuing night, and asked the Boston man to pray. The narrator said he had never prayed in his life, and could not pray, and was obliged to tell his host so; and the Fijian kneeled down and prayed for him. It seemed a strange reversal of the usual order of things—the Fijian praying for the American; and that prayer, the captain said, was the means of his subsequent conversion to God, and ultimately brought him to the foot of the cross. That sea captain is now a missionary to the heathen.

INDIA AND BURMAH.

The Cobbler's Idea.—How it was received.—Attempt great things for God.—A Suggestion.—Schwartz.—An Aged Convert.—A New Testament.—An Escape.—Hook-swinging.—Mrs. Wilson's first School.—Burmah.—Interview with the King.—The Death-Prison.—Story of Moung Moung.—The Karens.—Two Karen Preachers.—George Boardman.—Sarah Boardman.—A Burman Gentleman.—Devotion.—Another Interview between a Missionary and a King of Burmah.

THE COBBLER'S IDEA.

WILLIAM CAREY, who may be called the father of modern missionary societies, was the son of the parish schoolmaster in the village of Pury, in Northamptonshire. Very early he showed a taste for books, and a wonderful perseverance in acquiring knowledge of all kinds. At six years old he worked out sums in his head; he loved history and books of travels, and used to fill his room with insects collected for scientific purposes; and at twelve years old he bought a Latin vocabulary, and carefully committed it to memory. But his parents were poor, and could not afford him a good education; so that nearly all which he acquired during his life was by his own efforts. At fourteen he was bound apprentice to a shoemaker, and in his master's shop found a Commentary on the New Testament, which contained some Greek words. These he copied out, and carried to a young acquaintance who had greater advantages. Thus were his early studies conducted. The Rev. Thomas Scott, the commentator, who used to pay pastoral visits at his master's, was accustomed, in after years, to point out the humble cottage which he said had been Carey's college. A fellow-servant was the instrument of his conversion; and by the time he was eighteen he had preached his first sermon. It was while reading "Cook's Voyages Round the World" that the design of sending the Gospel to the heathen first entered his mind; and from that time it absorbed his thoughts. He had a large map of his own making hung against the wall, and on it he entered every particular which he could glean of the various heathen countries; so that while he sat at his work, he could muse on his great design. He never made much of his trade; and years after, when dining with the Governor-General of India, on hearing one of the guests ask whether Dr. Carey had not once been a shoemaker, he stepped forward and said, "No, sir; only a cobbler."

HOW IT WAS RECEIVED.

Two hundred years ago, in the times of the old Puritans, when the East India Company was only a company of merchants, the directors, like Christian men, sent out schoolmasters and clergymen, who were exhorted to learn the native languages, in order to propagate Christianity in foreign parts. But gradually the life of the Christian Church became weaker and colder, while the nation grew daily prouder and yet more proud, until after the battle of Plassy, which laid the foundation of our Indian empire, she had well-nigh entirely forgotten her God. By that time, even among the most part of Christian men, the Master's command to "go into all the world and preach the Gospel to every creature" had become almost a dead letter, —so much so, that when Carey, at a meeting of ministers, proposed, as a subject for discussion, "The duty of Christians to attempt the spread of the Gospel among heathen nations," the venerable president sprang to his feet and thundered out, "Young man, sit down. When God pleases to convert the heathen, he will do it without your aid or mine."

ATTEMPT GREAT THINGS FOR GOD.

William Carey had an ignorant, unsympathizing wife, whom he had married before he was twenty years of age. He had a colleague who, though full of missionary ardour, was so constantly running into debt, that he was quite a thorn in his side. He had to raise all the money necessary to convey himself and his family to India; and when there he found himself penniless, and reduced to the necessity, first of taking a farm, and then of superintending an indigo factory, in order to obtain daily bread. No such things as punkahs or venetians were in use then. He frequently had to live in unhealthy houses, and, at least for years, in the most economical manner possible. He laboured for six years without seeing any fruit; saw several fellow-labourers fall beside him; was ordered by the English Government to leave India; and then only suffered to take refuge in the Danish settlement of Serampore; but the motto of his first missionary sermon was still his motto for life,—"Expect great things from God; attempt great things for God."

The mission station of Serampore became famous among missions; and Dr. Carey lived to be renowned for his translations as well as for his evangelistic labours. By the year 1800, nearly the whole Bible was given to the people in Bengalee. It was followed by tracts, grammars, and dictionaries.

The cobbler missionary was visited on his death-bed by the wife of the Governor-General, and his blessing asked by the Bishop of Calcutta. The effect of his forty years' work among the heathen can never be forgotten or pass away.

A SUGGESTION.

To the kingdom of Denmark belongs the honour of sending the first Protestant missionary to India, and to Ziegenbalg that of being the first to go. He and his companion, Henry Plutscho, arrived at the Danish settlement of Tranquebar, in July, 1706; and before the year was out they had baptized their first convert, Modaliapa.

In 1714, a translation of the New Testament in Tamil—the work of Ziegenbalg—was printed. Other missionaries went out, and amidst considerable opposition, especially from the Romanists, the work was prosecuted with vigour, and with such success, that, by the year 1750, the converts at Tranquebar and the neighbouring towns and villages, and at Madras and Cuddalore, amounted to about nine thousand.

Now all this vast work, which has gone on and prospered unto this day, was undertaken at the suggestion of one man, Dr. Lutkens, chaplain to Frederick IV. of Denmark, who by him was induced to establish the mission; and who consequently applied to Dr. Francke, of Halle, in Saxony, to recommend a suitable man to send out.

SCHWARTZ.

When the mother of Schwartz lay on her death-bed, she told her husband, and the pastor who attended her, that she had dedicated her infant son to the Lord, and obtained a promise from them that if in after years he should show an inclination for the ministry, they would foster it to the uttermost of their power.

At twenty-one years of age he was living in the Orphan House at Halle, when Professor Francke first proposed the missionary work to him. The idea of the sacred calling, although new to him, was gladly entertained; and Schwartz determined to respond to it if he could obtain his father's leave. He started homewards; fearing, however, that as the eldest son, he would be regarded as the prop of the family, and that, therefore, his consent would be withheld. The father gave no decided answer, but fixed a day when, after deliberation, he would declare his determination. The whole family waited in anxiety for this day,—the young candidate fearing a refusal, and the brothers and sisters, a consent. At length his father came down from his chamber, and bade him depart in the name of the Lord; charging him to forget his native country and his father's house, and to go and win many souls to Christ. A few days after, an advantageous offer was made to him of entering on the ministry at home; but he had put his hand to the plough, and would not turn back. He had begun the study of Tamil, at Halle, with a view to assist in bringing out a new edition of the Tamil Scriptures; and within four months after his arrival, he preached his first sermon in Ziegenbalg's church. For nearly fifty years he served his Master in Tranquebar, Trichinopoly, and Tanjore; and Bishop Heber speaks of the number of his converts as amounting to between six and seven thousand.

AN AGED CONVERT.

An old man, said to have been more than a hundred years old, placed himself under Christian instruction, and, considering his extreme age, comprehended well what he was taught, and prayed fervently. Not long afterwards, when he was taken ill, he earnestly entreated that he might not be allowed to die unbaptized; "for," said he, "I believe in Jesus Christ." He was baptized, and, at his own request, named Rayappen—that is, Peter. During his illness, he begged to be read to and prayed with diligently; and when Schwartz visited him, the day before his departure, he said, "Now, padre, I am going to the kingdom of blessedness; and when I am gone, see to it that my wife, who is ninety years of age, may at length follow me." Soon afterwards he expired, and as an old man of a hundred years, and a child of God of a few months, he received honourable and Christian burial.

A NEW TESTAMENT.

"A brother officer of mine," says Sir Arthur Cotton, "in leaving for a time his works in a part of the country far from missions, selected the most able, active, and faithful native he had about him to leave in charge of the stores, etc.; the works being stopped while he visited Europe and America. With this man he left a New Testament; and, on his return, he found him fully established in the truth, without having had any communication with missionaries or other Christians. Though a man of good caste, he had openly declared his intention of being baptized, and had established regular worship on Sundays with any of the natives he could collect. As soon as he could obtain leave, he went to a mission-station and was baptized; and he continued to collect all who came to him in the evening and on till midnight; and when he had filled his house, he built a small chapel, and filled that also. He then gave up all his excellent prospects of advancement in the public works department, and accepted a bare subsistence as a catechist, that he might give himself wholly to mission work. My brother officer says he has never had a moment's anxiety about him. He has gone on most faithfully and devotedly preaching the gospel with great zeal and diligence. In this way God is now raising up men from among the natives themselves, and establishing indigenous churches throughout India."

AN ESCAPE.

"I recollect," says Dr. Duff, "the case of a young man who was married; but his father did not know it. He became a Christian. One Sunday afternoon he came with his wife to my house. She had never seen a European before, and was standing wrapped in a cloth, and appearing very

Swinging Festival in South India. p. 53.

timid. She had made up her mind to become a Christian. This being a Hindoo holiday, the house was left with only her and her husband and the servants; an idolatrous procession was passing along the streets; the servants went to look at it, and the young man and his wife seized the opportunity to escape. They were at that moment reading the 'Pilgrim's Progress,' and the passage they had come to was where Christian's resolution was taken to flee from the City of Destruction; and the wife said, 'Is not this our own case? Are not we in the City of Destruction? Cannot we flee too?' They rose up, found the doors open, and went out into the street; they got into the first vehicle they found, and drove as fast as possible to my house. They were soon after baptized, and are now burning and shining lights as Christians."

HOOK-SWINGING.

The Hindoos think it meritorious to inflict tortures on themselves; and one is by means of hook-swinging. The man who is to swing falls on his face, and another then marks two places on his back with dust. By means of smart slaps, or by rough rubbing, the flesh is a little deadened, and the hooks then thrust through. He then gets up on his feet, and is raised on a man's back to some height from the ground. The ropes attached to the hooks are then fastened to a strong bamboo lever, fixed on the top of a high pole, and the victim is swung round, while the spectators amuse themselves below. No sympathy whatever is felt for the man's sufferings; indeed, these occasions are considered as festivals! The devotee may swing a few minutes, or for hours; but he must not, on any account, show any signs of pain. Generally, some intoxicating liquor is drunk, in order partially to deaden the suffering.

MRS. WILSON'S FIRST SCHOOL.

In the year 1821, Miss Cooke, afterwards Mrs. Wilson, left England to devote herself to the work of educating poor Hindoo women in the principles of Christianity. She was one of the very first to enter on this field.

While engaged in studying the Bengalee language, and scarcely daring to hope that an immediate opening for entering on the work to which she had devoted herself would be found, Miss Cooke paid a visit to the boys' school, in order to observe their pronunciation. Unaccustomed to see a European female in that part of the native town, a crowd collected around the door; among them was an interesting little girl, whom the pundit drove away. Miss Cooke desired the child to be called, and asked her, by an interpreter, if she wished to learn to read. She was told that this child had for three months past been daily begging to be admitted to learn among the boys, and, that if Miss Cooke (whose intentions were known) would attend next day, twenty girls should be collected. Miss Cooke's efforts were crowned with success. The central school in Calcutta, which opened in 1828 with twenty-eight scholars, had three hundred in daily attendance in 1836; more than one hundred adults were baptized during that year, and about the same number attended Mrs. Wilson for Christian instruction.

BURMAH.

Sixty years ago, all Burmah was given up to the worship of the last of the Buddhs; in other words, all Burmans were atheists, and their highest hope was, not that they might be absorbed into the Deity, like the Hindoos, but that, if very virtuous, they might attain to the honour of annihilation. Gautama, this same last Buddh, has, according to their belief, long since ceased to exist; yet Gautama is the great object of their worship, and his laws are what Burmans are supposed to obey. But they are honoured only in word; for, while this code forbids crime of all kinds, those who are under its jurisdiction are a nation of criminals. This was the state of Burmah in the early part of this century; but since then light has broken into the picture.

INTERVIEW WITH THE KING.

There was a great panic, one day, in Rangoon; all the troops were under arms; and it was whispered that something important had happened. People were then obliged very often to whisper in Burmah. "There is a rebellion," said one; "The king is sick," said another: "he is dead" no one dared to say aloud, because the "lord of land and water" was reckoned immortal. At length a royal messenger appeared, bearing a royal mandate, and a crowd gathered to hearken. The proclamation was as follows :—

"Listen ye! The immortal king, wearied, it would seem, with the fatigues of royalty, has gone up to amuse himself in the celestial regions. His grandson, the heir-apparent, is seated on the throne. The young monarch enjoins on all to remain quiet, and to await his imperial orders."

The said young king had already murdered two uncles; and thus was a reign of terror ushered in. All knew what to expect. No innovation was to be allowed; least of all, a new religion.

But for some years past, Adoniram Judson, from America, a "religious making teacher," as the Burmans called him, had been living in Rangoon, and with him a missionary printer, and latterly two other missionaries. They had been diligently studying, translating, conversing, and preaching the doctrines of Christianity. One Burman had been baptized, and others were inquiring. The work had evidently begun, and to forsake it was impossible. No; "the business," Mr. Judson said, "must fairly be laid before the emperor." So, one morning in December, he, and one of his brother missionaries, embarked with a pass from the viceroy "to go up to the golden feet and lift up their eyes to the golden face."

It was the day of the celebration of a recent victory when they arrived at the glittering palace in Ava, and his majesty was to witness a grand military and priestly display. The minister of state received them pleasantly, and was engaged in putting questions touching their religion, when it was announced that the golden foot was about to advance. "Who are these? and why do you dress so?" he asked, eyeing the strangers intently; and having been informed, he said, "read the petition." It was one praying for clemency towards the American teachers, and entreating leave for them to preach in his dominions. The emperor listened, then took the petition and read it again. He next accepted a tract "adorned in the handsomest way possible." It began thus: "There is one eternal God, who is independent of the incidents of mortality, and besides him there is no God."

That was enough. A disdainful scowl gathered on the monarch's brow,—the monarch murderer. "There is no God" was the language of his heart, and rising, he dashed the paper to the ground. A beautiful volume intended as a present was adroitly displayed at the same moment by a friendly officer; but all was over. There was nothing but persecution for any who dared to confess Jesus Christ. Yet the voices of the few converts and of the inquirers held the teachers fast. "Do not leave us," they said, "until there are at least ten disciples; then appoint one to be the teacher of the rest, and the religion will spread of itself; even the emperor cannot stop it."

THE DEATH-PRISON.

It was a Sabbath morning, and the simple worship had just been concluded, when a messenger arrived with the startling intelligence that the English had taken Rangoon. All Englishmen resident there were instantly arrested; and as in the papers of one of them there was found an entry of money paid by him to the missionaries, an officer was quickly despatched to their dwelling. No sooner had the usual formula of arrest been uttered, than the "spotted man," producing the small cord, or instrument of torture, seized Mr. Judson and threw him on the ground. "Stay," interposed Mrs. Judson, catching hold of the executioner's arm; "I will give you money." But it was useless; the "spotted face" only tightened the cords so as almost to prevent respiration, and dragged his prisoner off with a fiend-like joy. To the death-prison he was ordered, where the Englishmen had been carried before him, and there, loaded with three pairs of fetters, and fastened to a long pole, so that he could not move, they left him for the night.

In that den of horrors lay, week after week and month after month, the saintly man, who had forsaken friends, and country, and home, for the sake of these tormentors. The foreigners were "strung" on a bamboo pole, which, with three pairs of fetters for each, kept them fixed in a row on the floor, without mattress or covering. They were nine in number, and so closely crowded together that the outside berth was welcomed with the greatest joy. When suffered to walk in the little prison-yard, it was still with the clanking of the heavy fetters—their ankles only a few inches apart—and, behind, the hideous guards.

To please the Burmans, Mrs. Judson had long adopted the Burmese style of dress; and it gave to her graceful person a singularly commanding air. By dint of continual presents and persuasions, she obtained leave to visit the poor captives daily; and on one of the earliest occasions, she and her husband had contrived a plan to save the manuscript of the New Testament, which, on account of the damp, could no longer remain buried under the house. This was to sew it up into a pillow so mean and hard that not even a Burman would covet it.

STORY OF MOUNG MOUNG.

Years had passed away, and Dr. Judson's incomparable wife and two tender babes lay sleeping in the dust; but he, set free at last, held steadily on his way. Crowds now came to the preaching at the zayat, and many souls had been granted to reward his labours. In one year, one hundred and twenty were added to the Lord.

Seated in the zayat day by day, the untiring missionary repeated to each new comer the same simple truths, or read aloud a tract written by himself, in the hope that some passer-by might be arrested, and enter in. There was one, a tall, dignified stranger, who passed constantly, leading a little bright-eyed boy. "Papa," cried the child, one day, "there is Jesus Christ's man." The father did not speak, but each day the child gave "Jesus Christ's man" a smile of recognition. "Is it true?" he asked, at length, looking up with a smile into the stern, bearded face, "that she, my mother, *shikoed* to the Lord Jesus Christ?" The father made no direct reply; but the missionary, hearing and seeing enough to interest him, called to Ko Shway-bay, a native convert, asking who this strange man might be. "Does the teacher remember," said the man, after explaining that he was a writer under Government, "a young woman who came here some three or four years ago for medicine? She had the face of a goddess, and her voice was like the silvery chimes of the pagoda-bell. She was the favourite wife of this sah-ya. Has the teacher forgotten putting a Gospel of Matthew in her hand, and saying that it contained medicine for her; for that she was afflicted with a worse disease than the fever of her little son?" Mr. Judson did not recall the circumstance. "What came of it?" he said. "She read that book at night, while watching by her baby, and then she would kneel down and pray, as the teacher had done. At last the sah-ya got the writing." "What did he do with it?" "Only burned it. But she was a tender little creature, and could not bear his look; so, as the baby got out of danger, she took the fever. The sah-ya was very fond of her, and did every thing to save her; but she just grew weaker day after day, and her face more beautiful, and there was no holding her back. She got courage as she drew near paradise, and begged the sah-ya to send for you. He is not a hard-hearted man, and she was more than life and soul to him; but he would not send; and so she died, talking to the last moment of the Lord Jesus, and calling on everybody about her to love him, and to worship none but him. It is not very safe to know any thing, for the sah-ya has taken an oath to destroy every one having too good a memory; but"—and the man looked cautiously around —"does the teacher think that little Burmese children are likely to run into the arms of foreigners without being taught?"

On the fourth day after this conversation,

who should spring up the steps of the zayat but the child, a light laugh playing on his beautiful features, and behind him his grave, dignified father! The boy had on his head a new Madras turban, which Dr. Judson had given him one day as he passed, surmounted by a red lacquered tray, bearing a cluster of golden plantains. The gift was placed at Judson's feet; and the father, with a courteous bow, took his seat upon the mat. "My little son here has heard of you, sir," he said, with an air of assumed carelessness, but betraying to Judson's practised eye a deep, wearing anxiety; "and he is very anxious to learn something of Jesus Christ. It is a pretty story you tell of that man,—prettier than any of our fables,—and you need not be afraid to set it forth in its brightest colours, for my little Moung Moung will never see through its absurdity, of course." "You think so," said Judson. "I perceive you are a päramät." "No, oh, no! I am a true and faithful worshipper of Lord Gautama; but, of course, neither you nor I subscribe to all the fables of our respective religions." "But what if I should tell you that I do believe every thing that I preach as firmly as I believe you sit on that mat before me; and that it is the one desire of my life to make everybody else believe it,—you and your child among the rest?" The sah-ya tried to smile, but only answered quietly, "I have heard of a writing you possess, which, by your leave, I will take home and read to Moung Moung." "Sah-ya!" said Judson, solemnly, holding out to him a tract, "I herewith put into your hands the key to eternal life and happiness." He added more, until the child suddenly exclaimed, "Papa, papa, hear him. Let us both love the Lord Jesus Christ; my mother loved him, and in the golden country of the blessed she waits for us." "I must go," whispered the sah-ya, hoarsely; but the missionary knelt, and said, "Let us pray." Instantly the child threw himself into an attitude of devotion, while, as the prayer deepened in fervency, the sah-ya's head drooped, and his face was covered with his hands. When it was over, he left with a silent bow; and each day, as he passed after that, a respectful salutation was exchanged; but that was all, save that, now and then, the child would run up to ask for a book, or to exchange a word of greeting, until one night, when cholera was raging in the town, there came a sudden summons for the teacher to go to the sah-ya's house.

Passing through a crowd of servants and relatives, he soon found himself gazing on the corpse of a little boy. "He is gone up to bloom forever amid the royal lilies of paradise," murmured a middle-aged woman, with a fan-leaf to her mouth; "and," she added, in under-tones, "he worshipped the true God, and trusted in the Lord our Redeemer. He was weary and in pain; and the Lord who loved him took him home to be a little golden lamb in his bosom forever." "And his father," said Judson, "his father!" "Oh, my master! my noble master, is going too!" "Who sent for me?" "Your handmaid, sir." "Not the sah-ya?" "The agony was on him; he could not if he would." "But how dared you?" "God was here," replied the woman, leading him into the next apartment, where, in the last painless stage of the disease, lay the noble sah-ya. Vain were his efforts to reply to Judson's expression of sympathy; he could not utter a sound. "Do you trust in Lord Gautama at such a moment as this?" inquired the missionary, softly, as the dying man seemed to make a gesture of adoration. The eyes were unclosed, with a look of pain and disappointment, and the heavy hands dropped on the pillow. "Lord Jesus, receive his spirit!" exclaimed Judson; and a smile flitted across the sah-ya's pale face. His finger pointed upwards, and a moment after he was gone. "To whom did he *shiko* at that last moment, mah-aa?" asked the missionary as, with the weeping attendant, he once more stood by the corpse of the child. "To the Lord Jesus Christ. I am sure of that," she answered. "But where," asked Judson, "did you first become acquainted with this religion, mah-aa?" "My mistress taught me, sir, and made me promise to teach her baby when he was old enough."

So was the missionary encouraged.

THE KARENS.

In a wild part of Burmah lived the Karens, a simple, artless people, who had for ages rejected the superstitions both of the Hindoos and of the Burmans. Groaning under the oppression of the latter, they spoke not of idols, but of God, to their children, and said that he would send them foreign deliverers, who would come by water, and bring with them the word of God.

Among these Karens a wonderful work has been done. They seemed to be a people prepared of the Lord; and when the Gospel was preached to them they gladly received it. Dr. Judson was the first to begin this work, and Ko-thah-byoo, a noted murderer, was the first convert. He soon became a native preacher, and had such great success, that an eye-witness wrote from settlements where, with the exception of one visit from Mr. Boardman, he had been the only labourer, "I cry no longer, 'The horrors of heathenism!' but 'The blessings of missions!' I date no longer from a heathen land. Heathenism has fled these banks."

TWO KAREN PREACHERS.

George Boardman had not long joined the mission in Burmah before he felt himself pressed to go among these wild people. Almost the whole of the first village which he reached turned out to welcome him, bringing presents of fowls, ducks, eggs, etc., and exclaiming, "Ah, you have come at last!" Ko-thah-byoo interpreted, and was engaged almost day and night in reading and explaining the words of eternal life to the people. Mr. Boardman was struck with his magnanimity, and said that though he did not in the least excel in intellect or learning, yet he was continually devising new and judicious plans for doing good. But preaching the Gospel seems a spontaneous act with the converted Karens. They think no more of the duty than a man does of the duty of eating when he is hungry.

One of those who heard Ko-thah-byoo preach was San Quala, the latter of whose names, signifying hope, had been given to him by his father on hearing of the arrival of ships manned by white men; for now he thought the tradition was about to be fulfilled, which said that white men should one day come in ships and break the Burman yoke from off their necks.

The glad tidings no sooner reached San Quala's ears than he welcomed them with joy, saying, "Is not this the very thing we have been waiting for?"

His mother had listened to the Word at George Boardman's feet; he himself had been a mourner at his grave; and thenceforth he was a missionary himself; and such a missionary as seldom is met with. Month after month, and year after year, sometimes alone, sometimes in the company of another labourer, San Quala traversed the jungles and glens of his country, carrying into every nook and hamlet the glad tidings of great joy. "When the teachers and disciples prayed in earnest," he said, "the Holy Spirit came down on the unconverted; and they came forward, requesting to be baptized. Many of these were people with whom I had laboured and exhorted before the meeting; and some had said to me, 'we will wait a year;' others, 'we will wait two years;' others, 'we will look on a while longer;' but, when the Holy Ghost touched them, they repented and became Christians. Many of those who had been among the unconverted came forward and confessed their sins and transgressions publicly They took up the habit of private prayer in the jungle, and became very anxious for their unconverted relatives. These things," continued this Karen preacher, "are the works of the Holy Spirit; but they are spiritually discerned."

There had been no written literature among the Karens; but Quala committed to paper every poem or story in verse or in prose, which he had heard related by firesides in the long rainy nights; and so Mr. Mason, having the words and phrases current among the people ready to his hand, was able, with Quala's help, to give these poor people a translation of the New Testament. Schools were established, and Quala said, "While the American teachers are with us, let us put forth strenuous efforts to learn; for should they leave, we shall be as orphans."

Then so earnest was the study that before many years had passed, the once ignorant Karens were almost on a level in intelligence and Christian knowledge with most Christian communities.

GEORGE BOARDMAN.

In November, Mr. Boardman and his wife set out for Tavoy. The hand of death was even then upon him, and he knew it; but it was his great wish to introduce a new labourer to his own beloved sphere of work among the Karens, and to witness one more ingathering from among the heathen. Besides, as he said to his anxious wife, he "knew beforehand that coming to a foreign mission involved the probability of a shorter life." Flocking from their jungle homes, the people hastened to meet him; and when they gazed on his pale, wan face, they shed many tears. "Sometimes," said his wife, "he sat up in a chair and addressed them for a few moments; but oftener I sat on his couch, interpreting his feeble whispers."

A motley group of nineteen Karens, who, a few weeks previously, had been in the darkness of heathenism, came in one evening to confess Christ by receiving baptism. In the evening, they all met round the table of the Lord; "and there," wrote one who was present, "in contemplating the agonies of the blessed Redeemer, I forgot the bitter cross preparing for myself." At length Mr. Mason arrived, and villagers having come to carry him, the dying man decided to start with him for the jungle. On the third day they reached the spot where, by the side of a beautiful stream, at the base of a range of mountains, a small bamboo-chapel had been erected. As the little cavalcade came up, nearly a hundred villagers were assembled, more than half of them eagerly waiting for baptism. Exhausted by the journey, Mr. Boardman no sooner caught a glimpse of the delightful spectacle, than a new vigour seemed suddenly to enter into his whole frame. Scarcely had they halted, when he was in the zayat, preaching almost as if in full health, and day by day, as the converts gathered to him asking for baptism, he conversed and prayed with them, until a reaction coming on, he was completely prostrated. "This poor perishing dust will soon be laid in the grave," he said to Mr. Mason; "but God can employ other lumps of clay to perform his will, as easily as he has this unworthy one."

The end soon came. Mrs. Boardman was eager to get him back to the city, where he could have more comforts. So the affectionate Karens carried their beloved teacher on board, and returned to bear his wife through the mud on the bank. Scarcely had she reached the boat, when the call arrived, "Come up higher." The Karens, according to his previous request, were summoned to watch his last breathings;

and in a few moments, without a struggle, he passed to his reward. The weeping converts knelt in prayer, crying, "My father! my father!" The first to meet them on their arrival at the house was the native Burman pastor, Moung Ing, who burst into tears. Reaching the sleeping-room, they uncovered the face, and gazing for a few moments on the placid countenance, on which still sat a sweet smile, the whole assembled group sobbed aloud. The next morning, his own spiritual children carried him to his burial, amid the tearful regrets of the whole community.

George Boardman's missionary life was but of a few years' length. He found the ground in some measure prepared by Dr. Judson's previous labours; and eleven months after his arrival, he was preaching in the jungles, where his great exertions, and the hardships which he had to suffer, brought on the consumptive disease which carried him off. But he reaped a harvest such as few missionaries have been privileged to gather in.

SARAH BOARDMAN.

An English officer on a hunting expedition from Tavoy was overtaken by a heavy storm in the jungle, where only here and there was to be seen some mouldering moss-grown zayat, when, while waiting at the door of one, he beheld, not many yards distant, among a party of wild Karens, "a fair, smiling face." It was that of Sarah Boardman, who, after the first stunning burst of grief was over, had dedicated her life to the service of those poor people in whose welfare her husband had taken so profound an interest; for Mr. Mason was still engrossed in the study of the language. So she toiled about, day after day, making tours through the country,—passing over swollen streams, struggling through the tangled jungle, and over craggy rocks and wild mountain-passes, while her child was borne by some affectionate disciple,—in order to speak persuasive words to those who still dwelt in darkness, or who had but lately seen the light. In Tavoy, and in the jungle, Sarah Boardman established day-schools, the care of which devolved almost entirely upon herself. And thus alone she laboured on until she became Dr. Judson's second wife.

A BURMAN GENTLEMAN.

The late Mr. Ingolls spoke Burmese like a native, as did also his wife. The Burmans are so cultivated and intellectual, that they take books and tracts with eagerness; and the Christian Burmans persuade every stranger to go to the missionary's house to be talked to, and receive books. One day, they brought a Burmese gentleman of such striking and noble appearance, that Mrs. Ingolls felt most anxious that he should meet with her husband, who was not at home; she therefore offered to lend him a book instead of giving him one, as she was afraid that if she asked him to come again, his suspicions would be awakened that they wanted to make him a convert; but she thought when he came to return the book, Mr. Ingolls might be at home. But on his second visit, Mr. Ingolls was out again; so she offered the loan of a second book, and when he returned that, her husband was at home. He was delighted with the book, and expressed a great wish to bring his wife to hear all they told him. He went away, carrying a store of books with him, and telling them that he should come again in a month, and bring his wife with him. Mrs. Ingolls was much disappointed that he did not come at the end of the month. At last he appeared, and three of his fellow-townsmen with him. After welcoming him, she remarked that he had not brought his wife. She saw he seemed as if he could not answer. At last, in great distress, he said, "She is dead." "Alas!" Mrs. Ingolls exclaimed, "then she has died without being able to hear the truth." "Oh, no," he said, very earnestly; "she is in heaven."

He then told Mr. and Mrs. Ingolls that, on his return to his home, he said to her, "I am not going to worship our false gods any more;" and then he began to explain to her all that the missionary had told him. But his poor wife was alarmed, and said, "Oh, you are going to be a heretic, and I will not sit with you." She then fled away into her own apartment. He tried in vain to bring her back, till, at last, to comfort himself, he sat down, and began reading his books. He read aloud by himself, and very soon he found that his wife was listening behind the curtain: for the women's apartments were separated only by curtains. She listened some time, and then she came out, and sat down by her husband, and said, "That seems a good religion; I should like to hear some more about it." He told her all he could; and the next day she was taken ill, and at the end of a month she died; but all that time she was hearing the missionaries' books read to her the whole day long. She had heard them over, and over, and over again; and she begged all her friends who came to see her to read to her; and the three who now accompanied him had become Christians through reading to this dying woman. Her husband is now a shining light.

The above narrative was written in 1857; and it went on to say: "The poor Karens and Burmans come hungering and thirsting, and they crowd the missionaries' houses all day long. Sometimes Mr. Ingolls and his wife could get no breakfast till three o'clock in the afternoon, in consequence of people flocking in all the morning." There are now a hundred thousand baptized Christians among the Karens alone; and they support all their own native preachers.

DEVOTION.

On the banks of the Sitang there stands an ancient city, to which the second Karen convert, San Quala, first carried the message of eternal life. It was now in the hands of Britain; and one day, as he was preaching, he was sent for by the English commissioner. "Teacher," he said, "I have spoken to the government that you should become a head and overseer among the Bghais, Pakus, and wild Karens, for which you will receive thirty rupees a month." "Sir," answered Quala, meekly, but firmly, "I will not do it. I will not have the money. I will not mix up God's work with government work. There are others to do this thing; employ them."

"Where," asked the commissioner, in amazement, "do you get money to live on? Why do you not like money? We will give you money, and you may continue your work as a teacher as heretofore. Will it not make it easier for you?" "No, sir," replied Quala; "were I to take your money, the wild Karens would turn against me." "Well," said the commissioner, "think over the matter a day or two." Quala went instantly to a Christian chief and another convert, and having persuaded them to take the office, he presented them next day.

This was the second time that Quala had refused the office of a magistrate. The work pleased neither him nor his wife, in comparison with that of a teacher. "If a man desire the office of a bishop," he said, "he desireth a good work. Why should I go back to things that are worthless?" Quala baptized not fewer than fifteen hundred of his countrymen with his own hand.

ANOTHER INTERVIEW BETWEEN A MISSIONARY AND A KING OF BURMAH.

The Rev. J. E. Marks, S. P. G., missionary in Burmah, had an interview with the king in October, 1868. His majesty received him in his palace at Mandalay, in which city there are more than twenty thousand yellow-robed Buddhist priests. The palace occupies an eighth part of the city; and on reaching the steps, Mr. Marks and his party had to take off their shoes. They were ushered into an apartment overlooking a garden; and in a few minutes the king came in. He had on only one garment, the pulso, or beautiful silk cloth covering from his waist to his feet. He reclined on a velvet carpet, near which the little prince placed the golden betel-box and water-cup, and then reverently retired. As the king entered, every Burman bowed his head to the ground, and kept it there. After taking a good stare at his guests, his majesty inquired whether Mr. Marks was the English poongyee (priest)? "He then asked me," says the missionary, "what requests I had to make to him, assuring me that all were granted before I spoke. I said that I had four requests to make: 1st, permission to labour as a missionary in Mandalay; 2dly, to build a church for Christian worship; 3dly, to get a piece of land for a cemetery; 4thly, to build, with his majesty's help, a Christian school for Burmese boys." The king promised to build both church and school at his own expense, directed him to get plans, and added that the school was to be for a thousand boys. He cordially welcomed Mr. Marks to Mandalay; said that he wished to place some of his own sons under his care, and professed his intention of granting liberty of conscience to all. Mr. Marks and five Burmese boys under his care were invited to breakfast.

The next day, when they found the king in his glass palace, attended by his queens and some of his daughters—he has ninety children in all—a pretty telescope was presented to him; and a box of beautiful needle and crochet-work, done by Burmese girls in Miss Cooke's school, greatly delighted the ladies. The king then began to talk to the boys, and to caution them not to change their religion lightly, and not to forget that of their ancestors. Mr. Marks interposed, saying that their ancestors had not heard the good news. The king seemed annoyed for a time, but soon regaining his good humour, he said, "I cannot talk with you about religion in public; we will talk about it privately on your return." He added, "Do not think that I am an enemy to your religion. If, when you have taught my people, they enter into your belief, they have my full permission. If my own sons, under your instruction, wish to become Christians, I will let them do so." "I could not help thinking at that moment," said

Mr. Marks, "of good Judson and his associates in 1823-4. What a wonderful change has come over the land since that time! May it not be that God is even now answering the fervent prayer of those devoted men in the time of their greatest peril,—'O Lord, open the eyes of the King of Burmah!' He was brought up as a priest; is learned and devout as a Buddhist; but he has not yet found peace. He is now earnestly seeking to acquire merit by the performance of good deeds."

CHINA.

China, and the Changes that have come over it.—Dr. Morrison.—Miss Aldersey.—Evil Reports.—A Young Convert.—The Story of San Avong.—Perils in the City.—Beggars in China.—A Text Unexpectedly Illustrated.—A Travelling Merchant.—A Prodigal Converted.—The "Foreign Ghost."—A Conversation about Confucius.—Buddhism.—How they told the Good News at Si-Pang.—The Praying-Machine.—Christians praying for Rain.—The Doctor Dzing.—Satchi-Hama, the Foo-Chooan Martyr.

CHINA, AND THE CHANGES THAT HAVE COME OVER IT.

It is now just sixty-one years since Dr. Morrison, the first Protestant missionary to China, landed in Canton. That great empire was, at that time, closed against the intrusion of foreigners, and, therefore, against the preaching of the gospel. The Americans had some commercial dealings there; so had the Portuguese, and so had the East India Company. But none of these had any right of entrance into the country; they were liable to be sent away at any moment, and only remained on sufferance. In the last half century, however, this state of things has greatly altered. Wars with England, and internal revolutions, have done much to break down prejudices; so that in 1843 the five ports were thrown open; and in 1858 the whole of China. But years before these things happened, the Church of Christ had begun to turn its eyes towards the land of Sinim, and to pray that the time to favour her might soon come. God ever suits his instruments to the work which they have to do. The first missionaries were men of indomitable courage and of untiring zeal. They were content to work on without any prospect of immediate success. When Robert Morrison began the work, his great object was to acquire this most difficult language, and to translate the Holy Scriptures, so as to prepare the way for other labourers at a more propitious season. In 1814 the first Chinese New Testament was printed; and in 1815 the first convert was baptized. But public preaching was out of the question; and for a long time the people manifested the utmost indifference about all religious matters. They were either Taouists, Buddhists, or followers of Confucius; but they could always be more easily interested by tales of the man in the moon, what he eats and what he drinks, than by any thing which had to do with a future state.

And then, having been, in a sense, a civilized nation for ages past, the foreigners had but few attractions for them. They had their books, and schools, and many of the arts, while Britons were naked savages; and all they now wished was to remain as they were. But a wonderful change has come over China. Not only is every town, city, and village open to the preaching of the gospel, but the willingness of the people to hear is quite remarkable. At least twenty Protestant Missionary Societies have sent missionaries to China; and the Holy Scriptures are being widely circulated through the length and breadth of this densely populated land. Moreover, the Chinese are at length convinced that all light does not flow from the "central kingdom."

DR. MORRISON.

Robert Morrison, the son of a last and boot-tree maker, was the first Protestant missionary to China. He was a member of the Scotch Church, and sent out by the London Missionary Society in the year 1807. No other person was found willing to go with him; so he went alone to his overwhelming work, though accompanied as far as New York by some missionaries destined for India. On the morning when he sailed from thence, they went together to the counting house of the ship-owners previous to his embarkation. The man of money seemed to regard Mr. Morrison as a deluded enthusiast, and when business matters were arranged, he turned about from the desk, and with a sardonic grin, said, "And so, Mr. Morrison, you really expect to make an impression on the idolatry of the great Chinese empire?" "No, sir," said Morrison; "I expect God will."

MISS ALDERSEY.

Miss Aldersey was one of the earliest Christian labourers in China. When only nineteen she began the study of Chinese, and at the same time endeavoured to accustom herself to hardships and privations with a view to missionary work; and in 1832, with her father's consent, she prepared to accompany a missionary party to the straits of Malacca, where there were many Chinese emigrants. But her heavenly Master saw that other training was needed for her; and when on the very eve of embarkation she was detained by the sudden death of a sister, which left six motherless children requiring her care. For five years she did her best to supply a mother's place to them, and when at length relieved from this charge, she left England in 1837, in company with Dr. and Mrs. Medhurst, and by their advice settled at Sourabaya, in Java, where she began teaching an Indo-Chinese school. For five years she laboured there amidst many discomforts, and then, with a young English girl whom she had trained, she proceeded to Singapore, where two of her baptized scholars followed her. She went on to Hong Kong, where she arrived on the very day when the peace was signed which threw open the five ports, and finally settled at Ningpo. There she opened a boarding-school for girls, first outside and then inside the city walls; and though it soon numbered fifty scholars, it was not until obliged that she applied to any society for pecuniary assistance.

EVIL REPORTS.

"We are now residing in the midst of a heathen city," wrote Miss Aldersey, a few years after settling in Ningpo, "and have to meet a storm of evil reports. It was generally believed, a short time back, that I had murdered all the children; and the mother of one of the children having heard that her child was dead, was permitted, of course, to see her, when she took the opportunity of drawing her aside, and gravely asking her whether she had not indeed been killed and brought to life again."

A YOUNG CONVERT.

"Atsi, one of my elder girls," says the same lady, "on leaving me a few months back, appeared in great trepidation in reference to a heathen marriage, which she knew that she would be expected to consummate, having been betrothed many years." This was on account of the heathen and idolatrous ceremonies connected with all marriages in China. "I am thankful to find," she continues, "from the testimony of many, that she was firm in refusing to worship the ancestors of her husband. Her relations and neighbours threw down the poor girl with a view to her prostrating herself; but she was firm to the end. Her foolish mother thought I had converted her into a Christian by means of medicine, and fearing lest I should get her under my influence again, in two days took her from the house of her husband and placed her under her own roof. There I grieve to think that she is badly treated by her mother and husband; both beat her, and the former burned her Chinese New Testament. I have taken care to supply her with a small edition, which she can conceal from her relatives."

Ning-po and the Mission Church. p. 87.

This poor young creature had long to endure much persecution; but her kind instructress did not leave her uncared for. She followed her to her home, endeavoured to win over the mother, and, as her husband was often away from home, got permission for Atsi sometimes to visit her, and to join in the Sunday services, and hold communion with the other young converts. "I sent a boat," she writes in her journal, "according to promise, for Sin Asan and Atsi. The husband of the former would not allow her to come. Atsi, waiting anxiously for my promised messenger, feared she would be too late for the service preparatory to the morrow's administration of the Lord's Supper. She got a young lad to accompany her, walking a distance of between three and four miles,—a long distance for bandaged feet. She is encouraged at home by finding two or three women who liked to hear of the religion of Jesus."

THE STORY OF SAN AVONG.

It was not long after her arrival at Ningpo, that Miss Aldersey was visited by a Chinese woman, who had some intention of leaving her four young daughters at the school. But a Scripture lesson was going on, and the children were so quiet and orderly, that she made up her mind that they were afraid of their teacher, and went away resolved not to do so. When some time had elapsed, however, she changed her mind; and returning with her husband, entered into an engagement to leave the children under Miss Aldersey's care for two, four, six, and eight years, according to their several ages.

San Avong was the eldest of the four, and nine years old when she first entered the school. She was a clever and amiable child, and from the very first gave promise of good. Her Bible soon became her delight, and its truths sank deeply into her heart. Her affections were won for Jesus her Saviour; and this was evident from her daily conduct. But when her two years' schooling had expired, San Avong was obliged to leave and be married to a heathen husband. She had no choice about this; it was the lot appointed for the poor child, and with a sorrowful heart she had to submit. Now, in every Chinese wedding there is one custom universally observed,—the bride is expected to prostrate herself and worship her husband's ancestors. By some means, however, Miss Aldersey succeeded in preventing this idolatrous ceremony from being enforced, and she also got leave for her young pupil to spend every Sunday with her, when they hoped to read God's

Word together. But on the very first Sunday after her marriage, poor San Avong was seized on her return home by three men, and, in spite of her resistance, forced into a prostrate position in the ancestral hall. "I have bowed down as a heathen," she cried, in her distress; "shall I be condemned with the wicked? Shall I go to hell?" When the Christian servants who had accompanied her were allowed to go to her again, they comforted her by assuring her that what was done against her will could be no sin. So she first closed her eyes in prayer, and then opening her Chinese Testament at Matthew x., read aloud from the twenty-fourth verse to the forty-second, and explained to her husband's friends and relatives why she had refused to conform to the usual custom. After this she was so greatly persecuted for refusing to eat meat that had been offered to idols, that Miss Aldersey, to shelter her, engaged her husband, Si Yang, as school-cook, on which he allowed his wife to resume her old place in the school, only stipulating that she was not to learn English. After this she was baptized, and for four years continued quietly to adorn the doctrine of God her Saviour. And at the end of that time her husband died; and her friends declared that his death was owing to her tears and lamentations during the idolatrous ceremony after the wedding. They, therefore, under the pretence that he owed money, proposed to sell her to pay his debts. In this extremity her kind friend again came forward, and by paying the fifty dollars required, secured her freedom.

She then at once began to study English, and soon became a most valuable assistant in Miss Aldersey's school. Her gentle influence was felt by all the children, and many owed to her their first religious impressions. If Miss Aldersey was obliged to be absent, San Avong would gather them together for prayer and reading; she helped in a working party, and translated missionary reports into Chinese, to read to the workers. For two years, also, she and a companion saved their pocket money to buy materials for an expensive piece of embroidery, which, when they had finished, they wished to be sold for the purpose of translating the Pilgrim's Progress into the language of the Samoan Isles, where they heard a good work was going on. But not content with her in-door work, San Avong used to take every opportunity of speaking to her countrywomen about the Lord Jesus. At one time she had a weekly meeting in Ningpo; but she soon was known also in distant villages, whither she would accompany Miss

Aldersey when she took missionary tours. Unasked, she unbandaged her feet, and when ridiculed for this, or for her words, she would bear the insult with such quiet dignity that often her revilers were abashed. Six years passed in these labours; at the end of which time, Miss Aldersey, feeling old age creeping on, made over her school to the American Board of Missions. On this occasion, San Avong sent her a present of a Chinese bag, accompanied by a most affectionate letter. At first she still continued to teach in the school; but as there was danger, in case of Miss Aldersey's death, that she might be forced to marry a heathen, she was removed to her house, and took charge of an infant school, which she managed to the amazement of the mothers who often found their children quite uncontrollable. In 1858, she was married again, and this time to a good Christian man, and a teacher. It seemed that a long course of happy usefulness was now before her; for she used to accompany her husband on his preaching tours, and speak to the women while he addressed the men. But on one of these tours she took a severe cold; and from that time her health failed. Still, however, she worked on almost to the last, though greatly harassed by her heathen mother and sister, who managed to get rid of her kind English doctor, and sent native ones to her instead. The mother also would taunt her with her new religion, and attribute all her sufferings to her change; but she said to Miss Aldersey, " I am happy. Jesus is with me." And to an old companion who had exclaimed, " What shall I do without you?" "Do not have an anxious thought. Go to Jesus in every trouble and difficulty, in every joy and sorrow. He is with me now, and he will be with you." "I am crossing the Jordan first," she said to her sorrowing husband; "you have yet to do so." Then she asked him to pray with her, but the poor man was unable to do so. At length she passed away, refreshed in the dark valley by the music of His name for whom she had laboured so earnestly. How many souls she had brought to his cross, the last great day only will show.

PERILS IN THE CITY.

It was some three or four years previous to the opening of China, that the Rev. J. S. Burdon, of Shanghae, and Mr. James H. Taylor, a medical missionary, resolved to venture on a visit to two islands of the river Yang-tze-kiang, and also to a city on the north bank, about a hundred miles distant from Shanghae. Tong-chow is a city of the second order in China, and the missionaries were forewarned that adventuring themselves within its gates in their foreign dress could not be done without hazard. The native teachers who were with them, and even the boatmen, advised them to desist; but, commending themselves to God, they resolved to go on. As they approached their destination, the possibility of insult and injury crossed their minds; but prayer to him who has promised to be with his people in the discharge of duty, encouraged them. Scarcely had they reached the gate, when a fierce, powerful Kiang-yoong, or soldier, in a partially drunk state, rushed, with a tremendous shout, on Mr. Burdon, and nearly knocked him down. In an instant they were surrounded by a dozen or two of the same sort, and amidst the most fearful shouts and horrid countenances, were roughly dragged along they knew not where. Wrenching himself from the grasp of the man who held him, Mr. Burdon so far outstripped them by running as to keep ahead of them, but his companion was most unmercifully dragged along. Mr. Burdon endeavoured to make the most of the dubious liberty still left him, and, as he went along, distributed his books; but the soldier, with the most violent gestures, snatched the books away, and called for manacles, to prevent this being done. Happily, none were forthcoming. "The books," said Mr. Burdon, "I had under my arm, and my carpet bag they attempted to seize, but in vain; I held on to both successfully. As they hurried us along, I began to suspect that they had no intention of taking us to the magistrate, and tried to ask some respectable men whom we passed the way to his office. The majority shrank from us as from a wild beast, but one or two pointed out the direction. We were taken through all sorts of back streets, and occasionally there was a quarrel among the soldiers themselves which way they should lead their victims. Whilst going along, one of the soldiers maliciously whispered in my ear, 'You are no foreigners;' by which he meant that I was one of the rebels belonging to Taeping-wang in foreign disguise, and of this my unshaven head was a proof. At last, almost fainting with exhaustion, our tongues cleaving to the roofs of our mouths from thirst, and covered with perspiration, it was the greatest relief I ever knew to find ourselves near some place, which appeared like the Ya-mun. As we were kept some time waiting, I got up on a step, and addressed the people, many hundreds of whom were within hearing. They astonished me by their quietness and attention; and there I preached Jesus to them, and briefly told them the object of our visit."

After considerable delay they were conducted in chairs to the principal place of business, and found it a pleasant change to escape from a rude soldiery into the presence of a courteous Chinese gentleman. By him they were kindly treated, and permission given to distribute their books, an escort being sent to protect them from further violence.

BEGGARS IN CHINA.

As to personal appearance, a more loathsome, disgusting set of beings could scarcely be imagined than the Fuh-chau beggars. There are thousands maimed, or blind, or sick; old, helpless men and women; young, tender, friendless children, who are obliged to beg for their bread. There are as many more lazy, degraded wretches, well able to earn their bread by the sweat of their brow, who beg from choice, and seem to like their trade. There is no such provision made by the Chinese Government for the support of the poor as is made at home. No poor-houses are built, no poor-taxes are collected in this "Middle Flowery Kingdom." There is a small sum granted by the emperor to each state or province in the empire, to relieve the aged and distressed who are without family or friends; but this sum is very small, and quite inadequate. As the result of this policy, beggary has become a fixed and acknowledged part of the Chinese social system. Beggars have their rights, their privileges, and, as a class, considerable power.

The beggars of Fuh-chau have a king, who has great, if not absolute authority over his numerous and truly formidable subjects. The son of the "beggar king" is heir to his father's throne and sovereignty, unless his majesty should name some other person as his successor. The method these beggars take to collect money is as novel as it is disagreeable to a stranger. Nearly every one of them carries a gong, or some such appliance for making a noise. With his gong and club, or, in absence of a gong, with his club alone, the beggar enters the store, shop, or bank, and commences his business by beating his gong, or striking the counter, accompanying the clatter with the most unearthly singing-howl imaginable. As soon as he receives what custom considers as his due, he leaves without ceremony, and goes through the same performance at the next door. But so long as the shopman delays to hand over the one cash, so long does Mr. Beggar beat his gong and howl; nor can he be driven away without his money. No Chinaman will, upon any account, strike a beggar; even if he should, the beggar would only stay the longer, and demand more money for the beating. If the shopman withhold his money, and continue his abuse, the beggar will take signal vengeance upon him by lying down before his door and starving to death, in which case the shopkeeper must pay the expenses of his funeral. The only way to avoid the annoyance of street beggars is to pay an annual sum of money to their king.

A TEXT UNEXPECTEDLY ILLUSTRATED.

One evening, as the Christians were all sitting round a table, listening to the catechist expounding the third chapter of Genesis, and explaining the temptation, the fall, and the first promise, "I will put enmity between thee and the woman," etc., suddenly the little company were startled by the sight of a large serpent coiled round the beam, quite close to the table, hissing with all his might at the catechist. All flew to the door, but the catechist brought them all back, saying, "Come, let us bruise his head, and then continue our meeting." So they set to, and succeeded in killing the serpent, and then buried him in the garden, and afterwards enjoyed their meeting, praising God for his kind protection from the serpent's bite, but, above all, that he had saved them from the power of the old serpent, the devil, in calling them to the knowledge of Jesus Christ, and giving them faith in his blood to redeem their souls from sin and death.

A TRAVELLING MERCHANT.

At Ming-ang-teng several men became interested in the truth. Among these was a travelling merchant, who was staying at Man-tea for a day or two. He seemed at once to drink in the whole truth, so eagerly did he learn. He said, "It is just the religion which suits my condition as a helpless sinner." He hurried home to tell his family of the treasure he had found; but his wife became frantic with rage at the disclosure that he had forever given up idolatry, and every thing connected with idols; and, to show her zeal and displeasure, she broke all the pots and pans, etc., which were in the house. This exhibition of her rage did not in the least influence her husband. So far from forsaking the truth, he determined at once to destroy all his household gods, and told his wife she was possessed of a devil, which nothing but Jesus Christ's religion could cast out. He told the glad news to several of his friends and neighbours: the result was that several of them came to Ming-ang-teng, a distance of ten British miles, to listen to the word of God. Three of those who came believed, and have, in common with many of their neighbours, sent a request for a teacher. In this way God is opening up new fields of labour for us.

A PRODIGAL CONVERTED.

There was a young man in Fuh-chau, who was one of the most forlorn reprobates for sin and crime in the whole city. He was guilty of breaking every one of the Ten Commandments. Though he was an only son, yet his father seriously thought of disinheriting him; but this had no effect on him. He seemed bent on destruction, and seemed likely to draw his whole family into poverty and shame. He went to the chapel, as people would say, by chance, and probably to laugh at the preacher; but God ordered it otherwise. He heard the truth. It laid hold of his heart, and produced deep conviction of sin, and a complete change of life. This change was the subject of surprise and speculation to the whole neighbourhood. This brought people to inquire, and at that time not fewer than two thousand books and Testaments were eagerly taken by the people. His father first doubted for joy; but after some time he was convinced that his son's reformation was real; and though he was a great idol-worshipper, he offered no opposition to his son in coming to the chapel, learning the books, and keeping the Sabbath. Several others were attracted to the chapel; and the young man became very earnest and anxious about his father's conversion, and appeared determined that he would not enter the church without bringing his father with him.

Ah! it was a spectacle worth beholding, to see that once reprobate sinner on his knees earnestly beseeching God for his father's conversion. Let it encourage others to hear that an answer was vouchsafed, and that without measure, in the conversion of the father, and his subsequent entry into the church by baptism on the very same day as his son and grandson: that son, once the plague of his father's life; that father, once the dark and most devoted idolater in the city, thenceforward help each other in the way to heaven, and cheer each other in the midst of much domestic persecution.

THE "FOREIGN GHOST."

In the month of November, 1866, the Rev. J. R. Wolfe started on a preaching expedition to the city of Hok-chiang, or "the city of blessedness and purity," accompanied by some native helpers. When they reached the town of Ek-tu, they went into a shop to rest and dine. It was immediately surrounded by crowds of people, anxious to get a sight of the "foreign ghost," of whom they had heard tales from their infancy, though they had never before the chance of seeing one. They looked at him half frightened, half curious; and when he addressed them in their own language, and told them not to fear, and that he was only a man, they seemed rather disappointed, and exclaimed, "He can speak: he is like one of ourselves." The shop-keeper was very kind and civil, and, under pretence of being so, placed him in the most conspicuous part of the shop. Mr. Wolfe felt that he was being exhibited all the time, but was quite accustomed to this kind of treatment, and enjoyed it tolerably well. A foreigner's way of eating is always a matter of great curiosity to a Chinaman; and on this occasion a thousand remarks passed on his knife and fork, etc. It was not, however, very pleasant to eat with a thousand filthy Chinese close around him, or to have his loaf taken off his plate, and handed round to the spectators for inspection. One man cried out, "Ten cash to see the foreign ghost." This caused a burst of laughter; but Mr. Wolfe pointed to the man who made the rude remark, and said that he needed to learn manners; and that if he was himself a "foreign ghost," this fellow was very much like him, asking which of the two ghosts was the best looking? This acted like an electric shock on the people. They laughed heartily at the supposed black native ghost, who hid himself away; and did not show his face again.

After this, the missionary was treated with more respect, and flattering remarks passed ón him. He knew etiquette, could talk reason, had wonderful ability, a tall figure, a white face, and, above all, he could speak "the smooth flowing words of the middle kingdom." For the Chinese are generally scrupulously polite and ceremonious, though they ask a number of questions of every stranger which would be deemed impertinent by an Englishman; such as —"What is your honourable name?" "How old are you?" "Where is your mansion?" "Are you married?" etc., etc. So these people begged the missionaries to forget the words of the "rough fellow who had neither sense nor reason," and not to think of their village as a place of no kindness to strangers. When they had fully explained their mission, and distributed books and tracts to the assembled crowd, they said that they were too tired then to preach much, but that they would visit them again, and teach them more about Jesus. A hundred voices shouted, "Do come again! do come again!" Before they left they had a private interview with one man, a literary graduate, and a person of some property, who wished to hear more of the doctrine of Christ. He listened with apparent interest, and received a copy of the Old and New Testaments, and a number of good tracts; after which the missionaries started afresh on their journey, very much encouraged.

A CONVERSATION ABOUT CONFUCIUS.

Wherever they went, crowds still came out to look at and to hear the "foreign ghost." But they were kindly treated, and generally attentively listened to. At one place the inhabitants sent to inquire of the catechist what kinds of food pleased the foreigner. The Chinese seldom or never drink milk themselves; but when they heard that he drank it, they at once procured some for him.

This was on the Lord's day; and after breakfast, finding a crowd of people ready to hear them, they proceeded to the centre of a large square, and, standing on a heap of rubbish, Mr. Wolfe preached from Matthew v. on the necessity of purity of heart, and told them of Jesus as the only means through whom it could be had. While he was thus reasoning, an old man came forward and said, "Stranger, listen to the words of the old man." He replied, "Venerable sir, I will hear: let wisdom flow from your lips." He proceeded. "I am an old man; you are young; the gray hairs have covered my head, and my eyes are growing dim. I have read the books of our great sages, and I love to hear of true doctrine; but what can be purer than Confucius? What can be wiser than his words? If a man follow Confucius, he can obtain purity of heart." "Venerable sir," replied the missionary, "I have read the sayings of your great Confucius; and I have read the sayings of the great teacher, Jesus, and I can tell you, that as heaven is higher than the earth, so Christ's doctrine is higher than that of Confucius. He was of earth; Christ was from heaven, and spoke heavenly doctrine. Confucius never pretended to speak of spiritual or heavenly doctrine. He was wise in this; for he was ignorant of God and of heaven. He was a great man; but there was a greater than he." I then pointed out Christ as the Saviour of the world, dwelt upon his incarnation, his life, his doctrine, his death, his resurrection, his ascension, and his present pleadings for his people; and then I asked, "Which of the two, Christ or Confucius, has done more for this poor, miserable, fallen world?" The old man still went on to say, that if a man followed Confucius, he could not do wrong. "I asked him," said the missionary, "to point out the man who ever did, and if he ever met with one, or whether he was sure that Confucius himself conformed to the letter of his own moral teaching?" The old man, after a little hesitation, said he never met a man who fulfilled the moral precepts of the great sage. Then Mr. Wolfe spoke of the powerlessness of all human teaching to change the heart, and make it fit for heaven, and said that Christ's doctrine was not human, but heavenly, and gives life to the soul by the Holy Spirit working on the heart. And once more the old man spoke, and said, "Foreign teacher, you look young, but your words are wise; your doctrine is good; it is deep beyond the understanding. Who is the Holy Spirit, and whose is the kingdom of God?" He listened attentively to the explanation, received a copy of the New Testament and some tracts, bowed politely, and departed; Mr. Wolfe bowing in return, and bidding him to "slowly, slowly walk."

BUDDHISM.

Buddhism is that system of religious belief held by the largest number of the heathen population in the whole world. Its followers are calculated to amount at least to three hundred and fifty millions of people, occupying the vast regions of central and eastern Asia, Japan, Ceylon, Siam, Burmah, Thibet, and Tartary in the north, and many of the Chinese. Gautama, the last of the Buddhs, and founder of the religion, is said to have appeared about 600 years before the Christian era; but he is supposed to have long since attained the honour of annihilation. According to the Buddhist belief, the earth is immovable, and placed upon a round mountain one million and a half miles in height, the earth itself being two and a half millions of miles in thickness, below which are three worlds of stone, water, and wind, each of incredible thickness. The Buddhist sun and moon are said to have been both swallowed up by a certain Assno Rahu, a giant of prodigious size, whose mouth is 3000 miles deep, with head and limbs of suitable proportions. The Buddhist priests wear yellow robes and are forbidden to marry; but they may lay aside the priesthood at pleasure.

HOW THEY TOLD THE GOOD NEWS AT SI-PANG.

In the course of one of his preaching expeditions, Mr. Wolfe reached a place called Si-pang. "We stopped at the first pong-taing, or hotel," he says. "The accommodations were, by no means, comfortable; but one is never disappointed in this respect in China, for one never expects comfort, and never finds it in a Chinese hotel. The catechist, the colporteur, the coolie, and myself, were compelled to occupy one small room, in which we had just space enough to lay ourselves down. The bed-clothes which are kept here looked as if they had not been washed for generations; and it would be impossible to count up the numbers who, from time to time, have reposed underneath these heaps of old rags. But their age is not the worst feature in these ancient coverings; they are literally covered with vermin, which, however, the Chinese seem to care little about. In the spot where I placed my own bed, I got the coolie to remove the Chinese bedding, and thoroughly clean the boards, and requested the landlord to bring me a new mat. My ideas of cleanliness and comfort only amused the people, and, no doubt, they looked on my conduct as the eccentricities of a 'barbarian.' After supper, the people thronged into a large empty space, to see and hear us preach. The people supplied lights; and I never remember spending a more interesting evening. They listened to the Word with the greatest eagerness, and when each of us was thoroughly tired with speaking, they went on begging that we should continue. I spoke twice, and felt wonderfully helped. I felt as if my tongue were suddenly unloosed; but the weakness of the poor body had to be considered. I thought I should never stop the colporteur; he seemed almost under an influence which he could not control, and I do not remember to have heard the gospel preached with so much clearness and impressiveness by any other Chinamen, as he preached it this evening. He continued till the lights failed; he complained of his heart being sore from earnestness, and yet he was burning with a desire to tell the people of Jesus. He is not a clever man; but this evening he beat us all out, and was looked upon as the chief speaker. Our books were as eagerly looked for as our preaching was listened to; and after we had retired to rest, an old man slipped a note under the door, begging for a copy of the book which talks about Jesus. Of course, such a request was granted by us."

THE PRAYING-MACHINE.

False religions are all alike in one respect; they teach, one and all, that man can and must do something to render himself acceptable in God's sight. The repetition of many prayers is supposed to be one great way of doing this; and to such an extent does this notion prevail in China, that there is frequently to be met with, by the roadsides, a sort of mill, known as "the praying-machine," into which passers-by may put slips of paper, on which are written prayers. Then just as many prayers are supposed to be said, as, by means of a handle, turns are given to the mill. This reminds one of the rosary of the Romanists, and, indeed, there are many points of resemblance between the Romish religion and Buddhism. The Buddhists have their convents and their monasteries, and in their temples there is frequently to be seen an image, called "the Queen of heaven."

CHRISTIANS PRAYING FOR RAIN.

The Rev. C. R. Mills, American Presbyterian missionary at Shantoong, writes: "The summer of 1865 will not soon be forgotten in this province. It was a time of fearful drought. The millet, beans, and corn were nearly all ruined, and the people were thrown into great distress. During the prevalence of this drought the poor heathen were constantly going in procession to the temples to plead for rain. At that time, three members of the Baptist church in Tung-Chow were living at no great distance off in the country. Two of them, men of moderate means, lived on their little farms, near a market-town twenty miles from the city. It happened on one occasion that these three Christians had come together for some purpose. As was very natural, they talked of the drought. While thus talking, one of them said, 'We are doing very wrong. These poor people, our neighbours, are constantly praying to false gods for rain. Of course it is all in vain. We worship the God who can give rain, and who has promised to hear prayer; we ought before this to have met together and spent a day in prayer to the living and true God for rain.' The others assented; and it was agreed that the three should meet at the village of the Christian woman to pray for rain. On the day fixed, the two men came to the house of the Christian woman. From the house they went out into the principal street of the village, and, having collected a crowd, announced that they were about to pray to the Christians' God for rain, and invited any who were willing to join them. At first the majority of the villagers were disposed to do so; but most of them soon turned away, and hooted at the Christians for worshipping the God of the foreigners. Some eight or ten persons, however, went to see the service. The Christians chose a service that seems to us very singular. They went up to the top of a mountain at about four in the afternoon, and spent the whole night in fasting and prayer. At sunset and afterwards they read the Scriptures and prayed together; at midnight and at daybreak the same, spending all the intervening time in private prayer. They continued their exercises until about noon the next day, having abstained from food about four and twenty hours. They then went and took some dinner with Mrs. Hong, the Christian woman, after which one of the men returned home; the home of the other being too distant to allow him to reach it that evening, he spent the night in the village. He started for home next morning, and was thoroughly drenched before he could reach it. The people of the village were convinced that the Christians' God gave the rain in answer to the prayers of his servants, and at first insisted on burning incense as a thank-offering. The conduct of these three Christians was quite spontaneous. So far from suggesting it, the missionaries knew nothing of it."

THE DOCTOR DZING.

In the year 1858, a Chinese doctor paid a visit to a catechist living in the city of Ningpo. The catechist's name was Bao. It was seven years since he had become a Christian, and since his conversion he had been a very active and able assistant to the missionaries: the doctor was Dzing Sin-sang, or Mr. Dzing. A few years before he had been struck with the thought of the wickedness of mankind, and with the great want of some hope of a brighter and better world to make them happy. He tried fulfilling the requirements of Buddhism, but derived no satisfaction therefrom. Some time after, he met with another doctor who was a convert to the Roman Catholic religion, and called him in to prescribe for his own sick child. This man got him to take a vow that, if the child recovered, he would examine into the doctrines of "the religion of the Lord of heaven,"—so the Romanists in China call theirs.

The child got well; and he not only did so, but soon embraced it. Now, having heard from his bishop that there were persons in Ningpo calling themselves Christians, who neither acknowledged the Pope nor worshipped the Virgin Mary, he called on Bao with the charitable purpose of warning him that his soul was in danger. But Bao knew better than he did the difference between their two religions, and proceeded to show him that though he had given up Buddhism, yet he had really taken up a religion very much like it; for that as his countrymen worship their saints and holy men, so do the Romanists worship the Virgin, the apostles, and many other dead people; and that by so doing they offer an insult to "the Lord of heaven," who, as the Scriptures teach, is the "one Mediator between God and man." Dzing Sin-sang paid several visits before he confessed himself in error; but when he did so, Bao took him to Mr. Russell, the missionary; and at length the poor man was enabled to cast away all those additions to the simple gospel, by which the Romish Church hides the light, and simply to go to Jesus as a helpless sinner, and receive salvation as a free gift.

After that, moved by the strongest of all powers—love,—he resolved to devote his whole life to his Saviour's service and to the work of bringing others to know him. He began with his aged mother, whom he had been the means of leading from Buddhism to Romanism, and soon had the happiness of seeing her a most loving and devoted servant of the Lord Jesus Christ, while other members of the family, most of whom had been baptized into the Romish Church, also joined the Protestant congregation, notwithstanding the opposition of nuns and priests.

The doctor himself took the name of Stephen, and, like his martyred namesake, he seems to have been "a man full of the Holy Ghost and of faith." He became a catechist; and went from place to place preaching Christ crucified with such vehement zeal that it was not long before his health gave way, and in the year 1862 he fell asleep in Jesus.

SATCHI-HAMA, THE FOO-CHOOAN MARTYR.

The Foo-Choo group consists of thirty-six small islands, which have sometimes belonged to China, and sometimes to Japan. The people speak a mixture of both languages, and are, in a sense, civilized. In 1816, two British captains visited these islands, and they and their people were treated with such kindness by the natives that they were not forgotten by their English guests; and years afterwards some of them determined, if possible, to begin a mission among them. In 1846, Dr. Bettelheim, a converted Jew, went as a medical missionary among them. By means of his healing art he gained the good-will of the people, and when, in a few months, he was able to address them in their own language, he was heard with attention. But the rulers soon became jealous, and his life was often in danger. Nevertheless, he persevered, and his labour has not been in vain. The people built huts both at the back and front of his house with a view to watch his proceedings. He did not object, but claimed them as a part of his residence, into which he had a right to go and put things whenever he chose. Among other things, he kept Chinese books in them, and the very guards stationed there received regular instruction from him. Satchi-Hama, who was one of these guards, an intelligent young man of about two-and-twenty, was soon discovered by Dr. and Mrs. Bettelheim, who were out together on a missionary excursion, confined in a dark prison, his feet in the stocks; and corded to a heavy beam, so that he could not change his position. The poor prisoner called to them as they passed, and told them that he had been repeatedly beaten by order of the Mandarins, that the worst food was given to him, and that gradually diminished; in fact, that he was condemned to an ignominious and lingering death by beating and starvation, simply because he had avowed his faith in the Lord Jesus Christ, and refused to recant. He begged the aid and prayers of his Christian teachers, and also some books. He said, however, that it was his Father who had bound him, and he would not rebel. A month after they managed to see the poor fellow again, and then he told them that he was said to be mad, and that these punishments and cruelties were called cures for his madness. He was then much reduced in body, but of the same mind. A month later, when they again made their way to the prison, the martyr was not there. They then wrote a respectful letter to the Mandarins, but no answer was returned. Every book which they had given him was taken away, and even every slip of paper on which he had written texts of Scripture. About six weeks afterwards they heard of his death.

NORTH AFRICA AND TURKEY.

Johnson of Regent's Town.—The first Convert.—Macauley Wilson.—An Evening March.—Affections set above.—A Welcome back.—Recognition of lost Relatives.—A recent Incident of the Slave Trade.—The story of Samuel Crowther.—Overthrow of the Snake Gods.—Mammy Hagar.—State of the Coptic Churches.—The Bible and the Monk.—An Abyssinian Evangelist.—A Ragged School in Cairo.—Seed sown in a Coffee-House at Cairo.—The Bible making its way in Turkey.—An Old Turk.—An earnest Turkish Student.—A Broken Heart.

JOHNSON OF REGENT'S TOWN.

In the year 1787, a little boy stood in his class at school, in Hanover, one Monday morning, while the master asked each in turn what he could remember of the Sunday sermon. "Call upon me in the day of trouble; I will deliver thee, and thou shalt glorify me," was all that William Augustine Johnson could recollect. The master was dissatisfied, saying it was only a text; and the boy, consequently, was so much grieved that he never forgot the words. Years afterwards, when he was a married man, and working as a day-labourer at a sugar-refiner's in London, while provisions were then at so high a price that often he had not enough to eat, he came home one day, and finding his wife weeping for hunger, these words came back to his mind. They brought to him, however, no immediate comfort; only strong conviction of sin, and of his unworthiness to call upon God. Nevertheless, when, after a night of dismal darkness, he returned to his home at breakfast-time, and his wife met him with a welcome to a breakfast which had been unexpectedly provided, a little light broke into his gloom. Not long after, during the preaching of the Word, his burden fell from off his shoulders; and a year after he heard the call to tell out among the heathen the loving-kindness of his God.

As a schoolmaster and schoolmistress of the Church Missionary Society, Johnson and his wife soon landed in the harbour of Sierra Leone, to which were brought yearly hundreds and hundreds of poor slaves liberated by the British cruisers. They were located at Regent's Town, where were collected together the wretched natives of twenty-two different nations, all prejudiced against each other, with no medium of communication but a little broken English, and in so degraded a condition, that if clothing was given to them, they could not for some time be induced to wear it. It was difficult at first to obtain scholars and hearers; but in a wonderfully short time this indifference gave way to eagerness, at least to learn and to hear, and the missionary's labours became so great that, from one week's end to another, he never had a minute to himself. Still, no mere improvement satisfied him; he wanted to see earnestness after spiritual things: and so long as there was no sign of this, he listened to their various requests in sadness.

THE FIRST CONVERT.

In October, 1816, Johnson wrote in his journal, "One evening, a shingle-maker, Joe Thompson, followed me out of church, and desired to speak to me. I was in some measure cast down, thinking he wished to speak to me for clothing. However, with astonishment, I found that he was in deep distress about the state of his soul. He said that, one evening, he had heard me ask the congregation if any one had spent five minutes that day in prayer to Jesus, or in the past day, week, month, or ever. He was struck with it, and could not answer the question for himself. He had heard the present and future state of the wicked explained, and he could answer nothing, but that he was wicked. After that, all the sins which he had ever done had entered into his mind. He had tried to pray, but could not; he would, therefore, ask me what he should do to save his soul. What I felt at that moment is inexpressible. I pointed him to a crucified Jesus, and tears ran down his cheeks. I was obliged to leave him, for I could scarcely contain myself. I went home and thanked God for having heard my prayers. The following week several more came in like manner to me; which removed all doubts and fears at once, and I had such an assurance that God had sent me to preach the unsearchable riches of Christ to the Gentiles, that there was no more room left for me to doubt."

Mr. Johnson soon after this received holy orders, by the desire of the committee, and was thus enabled to take the whole charge of his converts.

MACAULEY WILSON.

"Last Friday," wrote Johnson, "I went to Sierra Leone to attend the examination of the schools before the governor, when the doctor offered his company to go with me." This doctor was a man of colour, though educated in England, and known by the name of Macauley Wilson. "On the way he said that one Sunday afternoon I had spoken on the words, 'The blood of Jesus Christ, his Son, cleanseth us from all sin.' Since that time he could find no rest; he had often come in the morning in order to acquaint me with it, but had been kept back. Could I not give him some advice, for he had been notoriously wicked? I replied that I could give him no other advice than to come to Jesus: 'His blood cleanseth from all sin!' He has since attended family prayer in the church, and found comfort through that passage, 'Come now, let us reason together, saith the Lord; though your sins be as scarlet, they shall be as white as snow,' etc." This doctor was the son of King George of Yongroo, and had great influence with the Bullom natives. Shortly after, a wonderful awakening began at Regent's Town, and this doctor proved a great help in the work of the Lord. One evening, the missionary was detained unexpectedly at a neighbouring station; and when two hundred people assembled in the evening for their family prayer, the doctor came forward and took the teacher's place. Mrs. Johnson, who was present, said that he gave a most affecting exhortation, persuading the people to give their whole hearts to the Lord. So quickly did "the planting of the Word" bud and blossom, and breathe heavenly fragrance on all around!

AN EVENING MARCH.

During the second December after Mr. Johnson's arrival at Sierra Leone, there was to be an evening prayer-meeting held at some miles distant, at Leicester Mountain, where all the missionaries were to unite in prayer for the spread of the gospel. Many of the people of Regent's Town wished to accompany their minister; and at four o'clock, December 4th, they started, three hundred and twenty-one in number, to march through the mountains on foot with their pastor; Mrs. Johnson, who could not walk, riding on a horse behind. The evening proved one of heavenly refreshment; and as night drew on, they marched back through the mountain paths, the men and boys in front, singing, as they went, that beautiful and appropriate hymn, "Come, ye sinners, poor and wretched," etc., and the women and girls followed in another company, singing,—

> "How beauteous are their feet
> Who stand on Zion's hill;
> Who bring salvation on their tongues,
> And words of peace reveal!"

AFFECTIONS SET ABOVE.

One who had lately been effectually called from the depths of sin, when asked by the missionary, "Well, how is your heart now?" replied: "Massa, my heart no live here now,—my heart live there!" pointing to the skies.

A WELCOME BACK.

After a time, Mr. Johnson was compelled to take his sick wife to England. Many troubles arose during his absence, in consequence of the injudicious conduct of the person in charge. This person, however, fell sick; and Mr. Wilhelm, a missionary who came to take the place of the absent pastor, endeavoured, though vainly, to heal the unhappy divisions. Mr. Johnson's return was, therefore, eagerly desired. On the day that he landed, a negro saw him coming from the vessel, and ran off, winged with the joyful tidings, up the steep Leicester Mountain, along the toilsome path to Regent's Town. Mr. Wilhelm had just concluded the evening prayers, when a man entered the church, and, to the astonishment of the assembly, cried out, "All hear! all hear! Mr. Johnson come!" The whole congregation immediately rose; those that could not get out at the doors jumped out at the windows, and Mr. Wilhelm found himself alone!

RECOGNITION OF LOST RELATIVES.

In May, of 1822, Mr. Johnson was sent for to Freetown to receive two hundred and thirty-eight poor slaves, just landed from a captured slave-ship. Only two hundred and seventeen were able to accompany him, the rest were carried to the hospital. The scenes, he tells us, were impossible to describe. "As soon as we came in sight of Regent's Town," he says, "all the people came out of their houses to meet us with loud acclamations. When they beheld the new people, weak and faint, they carried and led them up towards my house. After they had lain on the ground, being quite exhausted, many of our people recognized their friends and relatives, and there was a general cry, 'Oh! massa, my sister!' 'my brother!' 'my countryman!' 'my countrywoman!' The poor creatures, being faint, just taken out of the hold of a slave vessel, and unconscious of what had befallen them, did not know whether they should laugh or cry when they beheld the countenances of those whom they had supposed long dead, but now saw, clothed and clean, and some with healthy children in their arms. The school-boys and girls brought the victuals they had prepared, and all the people, following their example, ran to their houses and brought what they had got ready; and in a short time their unfortunate country people were overwhelmed with messes of every description. Pine-apples, ground-nuts, and oranges were also brought in great abundance. Several had the joy to take a brother or a sister home." In the evening the church was crowded. A school-girl put some of her own clothing on one of the new girls, in order to take her to church. When the poor girl came before the church and saw the numbers of people, she ran back crying: she said she had been sold too much, and did not want to be sold again!

A RECENT INCIDENT OF THE SLAVE-TRADE.

A boy, the son of a chief on the Kittim River, Sherbro, was engaged, as is usual with youths of his age, in fishing. He was alone in his canoe, which he had brought to anchor, and was completely absorbed in his pursuit. A large canoe hove in sight coming down the river; there appeared to be many people on board. They hailed the boy, and told him if he had caught any fish to bring it, as they wished to buy. Unsuspicious of danger, and anxious to dispose of his day's spoil, he was soon alongside of them, when they violently seized him and

11*

dragged him into their canoe! Alas! it was full of slaves, of which he was condemned to form one. In vain his struggles; they overpowered him: in vain his cries; they gagged him. His father's village was in sight, and there were strong arms there and willing friends to put them out for his deliverance had they been aware of his danger; but they knew not of it. How could they? His cries were stifled; it was, moreover, far advanced in the day, and the shades of evening fell rapidly. The departing light took from him all hope; and as the darkness fell thick around him, he found his heart grow more sad and dark, for he who had been free was a slave-boy, perhaps for life. Cleverly was the victim caught, and the robbers rejoiced in their ingenuity, and mocked the poor boy's grief. Long and dreary was the night. He slept; but it was broken sleep, the sleep of sorrow, full of the remembrance of those whom he should never see again; and when he awoke, there was nothing around him save the wide, wide waste of waters. He sat silent and broken-down; for help, the help of man, was far away, and of God and his help he knew nothing; for he was a poor heathen boy. Ah, and poor Chow Boam was a very little boy, too; they might have spared him; but slave-dealers have no mercy.

Three days had passed away since they had left the Kittim River; and every hour brought them nearer to their destination; and then they should all be sold to the white man—when lo, a schooner hove in sight! Right well the slave-dealers knew her, and her mission too. She was British, and was one of the cruising squadron on the look-out for miscreants such as they were. The boat's sail was lowered; and they lay still upon the waters, in the hope they might escape notice. But the watchful glass, as it swept the waters, had detected them; and the schooner soon hove down upon them, and, as the water shoaled, the ship's boats were manned; and then commenced the chase.

Earnestly did the Susus strain and toil to reach the shore and bolt into the jungle; but the English boats gained rapidly upon them; and then did these bad men prepare for fight. Muskets, knives, and poisoned arrows were brandished in a formidable manner. But the muscular hand of the British sailor was soon on the neck of his prostrate foe; and the bound and pinioned slave-dealers found themselves dealt with as they had dealt with others.

Lieutenant Harger soon carried his prize into Freetown. The court pronounced the seizure good and lawful; and all the slaves were set at liberty, among them four boys and four girls, our friend Chow Boam being one of the number. He was sent to Regent's Town, and placed under the care of one of our missionaries, and there both soul and body were cared for, and he was tenderly dealt with. Poor little fellow! it was indeed a happy change for him, yet he could not forget those he had lost, and often wondered whether he should ever see them again. It must have seemed very unlikely; and he could scarcely believe his ears when, one day, he heard his name pronounced by a familiar voice. Friends had been sent by his parents to look for him. They had heard that he had been rescued, and it put joy into their hearts. The governor called Chow Boam before him, and dismissed him with words of kindness; and the boy left in a few days, his young heart bounding with joy at the prospect of soon seeing his father and mother once more.

THE STORY OF SAMUEL CROWTHER.

About one hundred miles inland from the Bight of Benin, lies a town, named Ashogun, situated in the Yoruba country. In the year 1821, this place was surrounded and attacked by a party of Eyo Mohammedans, who are constantly engaged in making slaves. A little boy, named Adjai, was taken prisoner with several other members of his family; cords were tied round their necks, and they were made to march, for many hours, away from their native place, until they arrived at Isehim, where each was sold separately. We will now follow poor Adjai in his wanderings. After being exchanged for a horse, he became the property of three people in succession; but the horse not suiting, he was restored to the chief who had bartered him, and taken to a town called Dadda, where he had the joy of once more meeting his mother and baby sister; but in three months more he was sent to a distant slave-market and sold to a Mohammedan woman, who allowed him some degree of freedom. A suspicion coming into his mind that he was again to be sold, and this time to the Portuguese, he made several attempts at self-destruction by strangling himself; but his courage failed each time. Then he thought he would, when he came to the water, throw himself out of the canoe; but when really sold again, and taken to the water's edge, the sight of it frightened him so much that he became stiff with terror, and could not so much as eat to the end of the voyage. Arrived at Lagos, his fears were realized; and he soon became the property of a white man, and was, with a number of others, put on board a slave-ship, intended to carry them across the wide ocean. But the poor little fellow's fears and sufferings were now about to end; for the very next evening, the slaver was taken by two English ships of war, the captain and crew put in irons, and the miserable Africans loosed from their fetters, and supplied with food and clothing. After cruising about for two months, they were landed at Sierra Leone, and sent to Bathurst, where they were placed under the care of a kind schoolmaster and his wife. In course of time, the instructions of these faithful missionaries were blessed to little Adjai, and he was baptized by the name of "Samuel Crowther." In 1826, he visited this country, the desire being then strong in his mind to become a teacher of his own countrymen. Soon after his return to Africa, the Fourah Bay Institution was opened, and he was admitted as the first student. In 1829, he married a Christian countrywoman of his own; and for many years he laboured devotedly as the schoolmaster of Regent's Town.

In 1841, he accompanied the Niger expedition, as native interpreter, and soon after paid a second visit to England, entered the missionary college at Islington, and in due time was ordained by the Bishop of London. The Yoruba people

Mr. Crowther preaching at Abbeokuta.

p. 131.

were then asking for a missionary; so Samuel Crowther was, naturally, appointed to this work. Whilst waiting, however, for a convenient opportunity to go to Abbeokuta with Mr. Townsend, he applied himself to the work of translation, and before the end of the year had finished the Gospel of Luke, the Acts, and the Epistle to the Romans. He had not been in Abbeokuta three weeks, before his own mother, from whom he had been torn twenty-five years before, came in search of him. "We could not say much," he says; "but sat still, and cast now and then an affectionate look at one another." One of her relatives had rescued her from slavery, and she had since then redeemed her daughter; but after many inquiries, Adjai had long since been given up for lost. The mother and daughter had been taken again, and again redeemed: indeed, theirs, as well as Adjai's, was a long story of troubles. Mr. Crowther's labours in his own land were graciously owned and blessed; young and old, chiefs and people, eagerly listened to his message. A church was built, and houses for the missionaries, and before long, a number of the natives offered themselves for baptism; and among them, to his great joy, Mr. Crowther's own mother, who received the name of Hannah.

The good work went on; many evangelists have since gone into the Niger country; and, in spite of desperate opposition, churches have been raised up here and there; so, in 1864, it was thought that the time was come to appoint a chief pastor over them, and in June of that year Samuel Crowther was consecrated as "first Bishop of the Niger."

OVERTHROW OF THE SNAKE GODS.

"A decided and most important step," says Bishop Crowther, "has been taken in the right direction, by King George Pepple, of Bonny, and his chiefs most favourable to Christianity, and a great downfall of one of the strongholds of Satan in this place. The guanas, which have hitherto been the juju, or sacred reptiles of the gods, and which have been worshipped, have been renounced, and declared, at a meeting of the king and his leading chiefs, on Easter Day, 21st of April, 1867, to be no longer Bonny juju. The consequence was that these reptiles were doomed to destruction. No sooner was this renunciation made, and orders given to clear the town of them, than many persons turned out in pursuit of these poor reptiles, which had so long been idolized, and killed them, as it were, in revenge, and strewed their carcases all about in open places, and in the markets, by dozens and scores. Fifty-seven were counted at one market-place alone, where they were exposed to view as a proof of the people's conviction of former errors and that they were determined to reform in good earnest in this respect. Wherever one went, the carcase of the guana met the sight.

"There was another decision made respecting the removal of the guanas. Lest any should hereafter say he had not had some share in the extinction of the sacred reptiles, it was decided that some of the blood should be sprinkled into all the wells in Bonny town to indicate that they had all concurred, not only in its destruction, but in its use as food. Many soon began to feed upon the flesh roasted with fire. This reminds me of the passage, 'And he took the calf which they had made, and burnt it in the fire, and ground it to powder, and strawed it upon the water, and made the children of Israel drink of it.' (Exod. xxxii. 20.) It cannot be expected that all the people had the resolution of the king and his chiefs to act fearlessly. Superstitious fear does not soon vanish away from minds long held by it; consequently, the wells of water were shunned from superstitious fear rather than from disgust. The water-girls poured suddenly upon us for a supply out of our well, in great numbers, with their pitchers on their shoulders, many of them in a state of nudity. Here was an opportunity for me to correct the evil of such habits, which I could not do in the town. Now I have made a strong rule that no one should be allowed to enter the mission premises to draw water unless clothed. Not only had the people suffered great losses by these reptiles devouring their chickens, but several persons had suffered, by being beaten or put to death, for hunting or unwittingly killing one of the sacred reptiles. Being thus protected, the guanas became tame, and ranged about everywhere, like domestic creatures, unmolested. It was believed that if any person should kill one of them, the vengeance of the gods would be felt throughout the country. God, in his mysterious providence, seemed to have made the late King Pepple's exile from Bonny, for a time, the means of paving the way for the changes which are now taking place here. He had it in his mind to do this when the mission was actually established here; but he had many prejudices to encounter, which time only could remove. He died without accomplishing this; but it was left for his son George, who has succeeded him on the throne, to strike the blow."

MAMMY HAGAR.

Mammy Hagar, as the subject of the following narrative was called, was of the Ebo tribe, and was brought into the colony some forty years ago in the usual way, *i. e.*, by British cruisers, and was baptized by the late missionary, Johnson. She confessed that then she did not understand the nature and requirements of the gospel; but she was wonderfully kept by God's grace; so that, from the time she was baptized, until her death, which occurred in December, 1865, she has always been a consistent member, and humble, attending to all the means of grace. Poor as she was, and a widow (for she lost her husband many years ago), and depending on the charity of friends, and the small Government allowance of twopence a day, granted to invalids and persons in her circumstances, she always managed to pay her class-coppers regularly every week for the pastorate, and subscribe her mite to the Church Missionary Society, the Bible Society, and, in fact, to every object brought before her notice in the parish. Three years ago she was brought near death's door. We gave her over. I felt deeply for her, because she was constantly at my house, and was like a grandmother to my children.

However, it pleased the Lord to raise her up, contrary to her own expectation and that of her friends. Her appearance in church, at her place, after a long and dangerous illness, was an occasion of great joy to all the members of the congregation, and hearty thanksgiving was publicly made for her. Still, she never felt herself all right again. It was plain to all that she was much shaken; and, in October last, there were unmistakable signs that the earthly tabernacle would soon be dissolved. She was missed in church, being laid by with severe pains and general debility. I visited her,and felt in my own mind that, with her, it was only a question of weeks, perhaps of days,—that soon her happy spirit would be removed into the presence of the Lord. It was now that Jesus was glorified in his servant. Reduced to a skeleton, there she lay on a mat, near the ashes—literally so,—the picture of a dying saint. Her sick-chamber became the scene of great encouragement. She said to me, on one occasion, "Heaven, sir, is not far off; heaven live here," pointing to the palm of her hand. "I want to go to rest." Then she began to repeat that beautiful text, "Come unto Me, all ye that labour," etc. "Heavy laden," she repeated. "Me, Hagar John, have rest. Glory be to God." All who were present, with myself, burst into tears. But she turned round and said to me, "Master, my son, why do you cry?" I replied, "We all envy you: we would rather say, like Paul, 'To be with Christ is far better.'" "No, no," she said; "my son, my master, you have work to do. I am going home: mind your work. See, Jesus near you!" pointing to her feet. "Hold on; patience,—without patience no man can see the kingdom of heaven." After a short pause, I replied, in her own words, "Heaven, it is true, is not far,—it is quite near." She turned round and said, with a feeling I shall not soon forget, "Master, it be far, far from the wicked; but near, very near to the righteous," pointing to her palm again. On another occasion, when I visited her, I read those beautiful words of our Saviour, "Let not your heart be troubled." As soon as I began, she took it up, and repeated in broken bits—if I may so speak—the first verse and part of the second, then the latter part of the third, exactly like one who never learned to read, but who could repeat bits of Scripture by rote. When she got to the end of the third verse, she said, with a consciousness of being perfectly correct, "That in the 14th of St. John, 1st verse, not so?" I replied in the affirmative. She said, "Jesus prepares fine,

fine room for poor Hagar, and fine, fine clothes; no trouble, no pain, no crying, no sin, for ever and ever, Amen." After this she seemed to wish not to be disturbed, being in constant communion with God. Thus, after a few days of weariness and suffering, she fell asleep,—for it was a falling asleep in Jesus. A large company of Christian friends followed her remains to the grave, thanking God for having delivered our sister from the miseries of this world, and given her such bright hopes of an immortality beyond. Could Mohammedanism do this? Could infidelity? But this is only one of the many results of missionary labour.

STATE OF THE COPTIC CHURCHES.

It was about the year 1828, when Mr. Lieder proceeded to Egypt, on a mission to the degraded and ignorant Coptic Christians of that down-trodden land. Christianity is supposed, by many, to have been first preached there by Mark; and it is known to have had many adherents, from the days immediately succeeding the apostles; but at the present time, the Coptic Church needs a missionary as much almost as any heathen community. In one of the churches, the priests showed to Mr. Lieder a little cross, made of silver, and said: "With this we drive away the devil." They administer the Lord's Supper generally every Sunday in their churches—but only the bread—and every one who wishes may partake of it; but the wine is received by only a few whom the priests think worthy of it; with these they go into a separate room, and give them two or three spoonfuls of wine. The bread may be received without preparation, but not so the wine; if any person wishes to partake of this, he is obliged to fast some days before and after, and is to abstain from spitting for several hours!

In Medineh, two schools were visited, in the first of which the schoolmaster was blind, so that the children just learned a few prayers and passages of the Scriptures by heart, and only a small number of them learned to read by the help of a deacon. In the second, the master was not quite blind; but still, for the want of books, the children only learned a little by heart; yet these ignorant, blind schoolmasters were the deans of the church.

THE BIBLE AND THE MONK.

The late Earl of Aberdeen, better known as Lord Haddo, being in bad health, was ordered by his physicians to take a voyage up the Nile.

Touched with pity for the benighted inhabitants of Egypt, he determined to make use of the opportunity for distributing Bibles among them; and through Monsur, a Scripture-reader, some were sent even farther into the country than he himself penetrated. In this way a Bible fell into the hands of a monk, who, soon after, left his convent, and travelled all the way to Cairo, in order to place himself under the instruction of the American missionaries. Being enlightened himself, he was anxious to enlighten others. His name was Makar; he was a nephew of the bishop, and so great was the influence of his teaching, that a letter was written by such of the monks as were "zealous for the tradition of the fathers," to the Coptic Patriarch at Cairo, stating that sixty families had become Protestants in one town only, and petitioning him to interpose and crush the new sect. The number was probably exaggerated; but many persons had no doubt embraced the faith, both men and women; and after due examination into the subject, Makhiel, a native convert, was ordained to the charge of this little company of believers.

AN ABYSSINIAN EVANGELIST.

This Makhiel's history was a remarkable one. When fifteen years old, he had entered the

View on the Nile. p. 141.

Syrian convent of the Virgin Mary, in Nitria, and there painfully and laboriously spent much of the night, as well as day, in superstitious worship of the Virgin Mary. Quite illiterate at first, he got one of the monks, who could read, to teach him his letters; then he advanced himself, by his own assiduity, till he could read well, when he learned the whole of the Psalms by heart, to repeat before the Virgin's picture. The first gleams of religious light broke on him during his perusal of an old MS. in the convent, written by a Syrian mystic of the thirteenth century, called, "The Book of the Religious Sheikh," which is somewhat in the style of Rutherford's letters. Then, one of the monks who had been at Cairo, having brought from Messrs. Lieder and Kruse's mission a copy of the Bible in Arabic, Makhiel, being moneyless, gave for it a new pair of shoes, which he then happened to possess. Hence, gradually, but as yet only quite partially, came a further advance of his mind in religious knowledge. Going some time after to Cairo, he saw something of Mr. Kruse, but still with not much effect towards his more perfect enlightenment.

After his return to his convent, a new and young bishop to the Abyssinian church having been appointed by the Coptic Patriarch at

Cairo, Makhiel was called on to go into Abyssinia with him as a kind of secretary. In that country he spent seven years, during which he thoroughly mastered the Ethiopic, and thus became, in that respect, fitted for future evangelistic work in Abyssinia. But while there, he strangely mixed himself up with the revolutionary wars and political intrigues, which ended in the establishment of the renowned Theodore on the throne. The excellent missionary, Kraff, happening to come there, he so maligned him for his rejection of Mariolatry, that he was the means of forcing him to leave the country.

At length, in consequence of a political difference with his bishop, Makhiel was by him first imprisoned and then sent, an outcast and an exile, to travel barefoot over the rugged Abyssinian mountains to the Red Sea and Aden. Thence sailing to Cario, he at length came into more intimate connection with certain Protestant converts, became fully convinced and converted, and avowing his Protestantism, he was first cruelly beaten by command of the Bishop of Cairo, and then excommunicated. Alone, friendless, and in want, he after awhile went to the American missionaries in that city, and after further instruction by them, was sent to act as their colporteur and evangelist in Alexandria, where being less known, the prejudice against him as excommunicated was not so likely to interfere with his usefulness. At length, after three years of earnest, consistent, and effective evangelistic work, he was lent by the American brethren to Lord Haddo, as one of fully proved character, to act under him in the same kind of work.

A RAGGED SCHOOL IN CAIRO.

Going to reside for a time in Cairo, some few years ago, Miss Whately determined to do what she could for her poor Eastern sisters. She had been used to ragged schools in Dublin, and determined, if possible, to establish one in this neglected place. The very idea was laughed at even by those who wished well to the people. "Copts might possibly come," they said, "but Moslems never." She determined, with the help of God, to have both, and trusting to the power of his Word to draw and keep them, she only answered, "Time will show."

A poor Syrian family occupied part of the house in which the school was to be held; and the eldest daughter, a girl of thirteen, was to be the only assistant. The little room was made ready, a few prints and texts in Arabic fastened against the walls; a work-basket was stocked, and alphabet cards provided; and then an expedition made in search of pupils. Dirty as they were (for Egyptian children are often kept so to avoid the evil eye), they were won by caresses as well as kind words; and on the first morning, nine little girls, all Moslems, might have been seen seated in a semicircle, to the great delight of their kind instructress. By dint of infinite patience and painstaking, that school has gone on and increased; and it is at this time but the centre of various instrumentalities for carrying the gospel among the very lowest classes of this lowest of all the kingdoms of the earth.

SEED SOWN IN A COFFEE-HOUSE AT CAIRO.

The story-teller in an oriental coffee-house is an important person. Every evening he is expected to attend and recite long ballads about "Antar," and "Abou Zeid," or to relate some of the wondrous tales of "the thousand and one nights." One of these coffee-houses was so close under Miss Whately's[1] window, that she could frequently detect what was read. And she found that not only was it the custom for

1 See Miss Whately's "Child-Life in Egypt," and her "Story of a Diamond," both published by the American Sunday-school Union.

all present who could afford it to give a trifle, but that any good-natured person of wealth who lived near would frequently send his contribution, in which case the donor could always ask for any story he chose, unless some one else had been beforehand with him. The idea at once struck her, that, by this means, an entrance might be gained for an Arabic Testament. By the hand of the servant it was sent; and in great anxiety the sender planted herself by the window to listen for the result. It might be a fruitless effort, or one attended by unpleasant results to herself, she thought; but it had been made in faith, and the consequences were left to God. It was not long before the welcome words of the second chapter of Matthew's gospel reached her ears; and five-and-twenty men, who probably had never listened to a chapter of the Bible before, remained quietly and attentively listening even beyond their usual time. This reading was carried on, with some interruptions, for several months.

THE BIBLE MAKING ITS WAY IN TURKEY.

Not far from B—— there is a Turkish village. One of its inhabitants had purchased a Bible at B——, and, having returned home, was in the habit of reading portions of it to some of his neighbours. One day, whilst thus occupied, an Imam suddenly appeared in the midst of the circle who were listening to him; and the following conversation ensued:—"What are you reading there?" asked the priest of the Koran. "The Law and the Gospel," answered the possessor of the sacred volume. "You are wrong. I know that at Stamboul (Constantinople) many read that book, but all those who do so become infidels?" "But why so? is it not a good book?" "Yes; there are many good things found in it, which its authors have taken from the Koran, and inserted in it; but if you read it, I forewarn you that you will all become infidels." "May Allah preserve us from becoming so! If it be so, we will no longer read it; but what must I do?" "Sell it as waste paper to the shopkeeper." This counsel was followed; and from that day the leaves of the Bible served to envelop the pepper and cheese of the village shopkeeper. But, while thus employed, one of the pages fell entire into the hands of a woman who knew how to read. Struck by the words she there read, this woman called her servant, and examined her as to where the paper came from, and sent her to purchase several articles at the shop, asking that they should be enveloped in paper of the same sort.

But, not content with doing so, and learning that there yet remained a tolerably large quantity of the paper (a Turkish Bible forms a thick volume), she sent to buy all that remained of it. Some days afterwards, the shopkeeper, who found the business profitable, presented himself at the Bible depôt opened at B——, and wished to purchase a Turkish Bible. The agent of the Society, who had heard a rumour of the affair, asked what he wished to do with it. "I wish to make use of it to tie up my parcels in," innocently answered the shopkeeper. "Well," said the agent, "I cannot sell it for such a purpose; it is a sacred book; it is the Word of God; and it should be treated with more respect." The shopkeeper persisted, and offered to pay forty piastres for the book; but the agent refused. "I cannot," said he, "for any sum sell you that book, to be treated with such contempt." Thus repulsed, the shopkeeper departed, but a little later returned. On his promise that he would not make such use of it, the Bible was given to him for forty piastres. He had most probably found a way to dispose of it; for it is known that it was not in his possession, and that no article purchased from him was enveloped in its pages; but it is not discovered how he disposed of it.

The Rev. Mr. Williams, one of the first Mohammedan converts, who was once banished for his religion, and now preaches the gospel to a congregation of Turks every Sunday, was recently on board one of the steamboats that ply up and down the Bosphorus. Some Turkish soldiers were also on board. As Mr. Williams was reading his Bible, one of the soldiers approached, and said, "Do you read the Bible? So do I;" and sat down beside him. Soon another soldier, observing that they were reading the Bible, came up and sat with them also. (This account was sent in 1860.)

Recently, a Turk was looking at a Bible offered for sale at one of the mosques, and hesitating whether to buy it or not, when a Turkish woman, passing by, said to him, "It is a good book; my son bought one some time ago, and we sit and read it every evening, and we like it very much. Buy it."

AN OLD TURK.

"Last week," wrote one from Constantinople, in March, 1860, "the missionaries held a meeting for the purpose of examining a Turk who was desirous of professing Christ. He was an old man, nearly seventy years of age. He had been a Mollah, or Mohammedan priest, and, till within the last few months, a bigoted follower of the false prophet. He now seems to sit at the feet of Christ with the humility of a child. The examination was conducted in Turkish, and the old man's answers plainly showed that he had a good knowledge of the gospel, and of the great plan of redemption by Christ alone. He was baptized last Sunday, and now is identified with the followers of the truth. Three others were baptized about six weeks ago,—one the nephew of a pasha. His uncle has forbidden him to enter the house again; but he says, notwithstanding the persecution of his friends, he is very happy. He says he reads in the Bible that 'those who leave father and mother, sisters and brothers, for the kingdom of God's sake, shall receive a hundred-fold in this present life, and in the world to come life everlasting.' And this, he says, he is receiving every day, and every thing he needs, for Christ is all in all."

AN EARNEST TURKISH STUDENT.

A missionary at Sivas, in Asiatic Turkey, has lately written: "I am much pleased with our three young men from Marsovan (the seminary), who have completed their first year, and come to spend their vacation in our field. One of them is especially promising. He seems ready to make any sacrifice, if he may but preach the gospel. A year ago last summer, when I was at Gurun, he came to me, saying that his mother and brothers were provided for, and entreated that I would secure a place for him in the school at Marsovan. I asked, 'Why do you wish to go to school?' 'That I may prepare myself to preach Christ,' was his reply. 'But,' said I, 'money is necessary to pay your expenses; where will that come from?' He answered, 'You see this suit of clothes that I have on. They are old, it is true,' (I had seldom seen a poorer suit;) 'but by mending I can wear them for a long time. I have also another suit for Sundays, and a few tools. These I can sell for 100 piastres (four dollars), which will be sufficient for my books at present; and will also provide me with bread for a little while. When that is gone I know that God will give me work that I may earn more, because I have given myself and all I have to him.' After some further conversation, I told him he might go to Sivas, and remain there at school until spring, when it would be evident whether he ought to go to Marsovan or not. He went to Sivas in a few days; in March was received into the church; and in a short time after entered the theological school at Marsovan. For some days he has been providentially detained at Sivas; and as I have watched his course, and heard his earnest words, it has occurred to me that I ought not to say my missionary life has been a failure, if I had no other fruit to show than this young man."

A BROKEN HEART.

Dr. Grant and his associates were one day busily writing for the post, when the wife of a respectable Mohammedan merchant brought in her only child for medicine. They lived close by, and, as she came frequently, she ventured in unattended. Her appearance was unusually prepossessing. She could not have been over thirty years of age, and her little boy was not far from ten. Dr. Grant was so busy that he did not, at first, attend to her; and, leading forward the invalid, she began to plead for him with tears, saying, among other things, "He is all I have in the world." "What!" said the doctor, "have you forgotten your husband?" "Husband!" she repeated; "Can a husband love? He is a stranger to me, and I to him. Ah! the religion of Jesus is better than Islam; it does not tolerate such things as ours." The truth was, he had married others since her, and she was cast aside, while the attention once lavished on her was now transferred to her younger rivals; and these did all they could to embitter an existence already almost unsupportable. She was retained only for the sake of her son; and on him now centred all her love. But even he had been trained to despise her; and all the while she was pleading for him with a mother's earnestness, he was mocking, insulting, and, with a domineering air, ordering her to be silent. After the doctor had attended to him, she began to tell her own ailments; but he could only reply, "I have no medicine for a broken heart."

SOUTH AFRICA AND MADAGASCAR.

Cruelty of the Heathen.—Rapid House-Building.—"The Dead must not Arise."—A Christian's Sorrow for Heathen Relatives.—An Aged Sinner Converted.—A Kaffir Church.—A Kaffir Preacher.—The Gospel Rejected.—Good News from South-East Africa.—The Commencement of the Missions in Madagascar.—The Midnight Meeting.—The Proto-Martyr. Penalties for the Profession of Christianity.—Two great Executions.—Thirsting for God's Word.—A Long Journey for a Bible.—The Morning of Joy.—Heathen Malagasy.—Of One Mind.—Opening of the Second Memorial Church.

CRUELTY OF THE HEATHEN.

THE celebrated Robert Moffat, who has laboured for so many years among some of the wild tribes of South Africa, was once returning from a journey, and in search of water. It was in a part of the country where they could not expect to find any traces of human inhabitants; and, therefore, the sudden appearance of a little smoke was a welcome sight. On reaching the spot whence it proceeded, they, however, only beheld an object of heart-rending distress. It was a venerable-looking old woman, a living skeleton, sitting with her head leaning on her knees. She seemed terrified at their appearance; but Mr. Moffat endeavoured to soothe her fears, and said to her, "My mother, fear not; we are friends, and will do you no harm." It was long before she gained courage to speak; but at length, in answer to his inquiry who she was, she replied, "I am a woman; I have been here four days; my children have left me here to die." "Your children!" he exclaimed. "Yes," she said, pointing with her hand to the distant hills, "my own children, three sons and two daughters; they have gone to yonder blue mountain, and have left me to die." "And pray why did they leave you?" he inquired. Spreading out her hands, she said, "I am old, you see, and I am no longer able to serve them; when they kill game, I am too feeble to help in carrying home the flesh; I am not able to gather wood to make a fire, and I cannot carry their children on my back, as I used to do." This last sentence was more than Mr. Moffat could bear. Though his tongue was cleaving to the roof of his mouth from thirst, it opened a fountain of tears. He said that he wondered she should have escaped the lions; but she took hold of the loose skin of her arm, and said, "I hear the lions; but there is nothing on me that they would eat; there is no flesh for them to scent."

They tried to persuade her to go with them, but she was convulsed with terror at the sight of the wagon, and said, "It is our custom; I am nearly dead; I do not want to die again." They could only give her a supply of meat, some tobacco, a knife, and a good supply of fuel, and bidding her keep up a fire to scare away the wild beasts, had to leave her thus, promising to return in two days. When they did so, she was gone! but they heard, afterwards, that her children had returned expecting to find only mangled remains; and that hearing the story of the stranger's kindness, they had taken her home again, because they dreaded the vengeance of the great chief.

RAPID HOUSE-BUILDING.

On the 26th of January, 1818, Mr. Moffat arrived at the kraal of the chief, Christian Africaner. This man had once been the terror of the whole country; and for his crimes he had been outlawed from the Cape territory; but he had recently joined the mission and been baptized; and when he heard that Mr. Moffat was the missionary promised by the directors in London, he was much pleased, and said that, as he was young, he hoped that he would long live with him and his people. He then ordered a number of women to come; and, much to the surprise of the new teacher, they soon appeared, bearing bundles of native mats, and long sticks, like fishing-rods. Africaner, pointing to a spot of ground, said, "There you must build a house for the missionary." A circle was instantly formed; and the women, evidently delighted with the job, fixed the poles, tied them down in the hemispheric form, and covered them with the mats, all ready for habitation, in the course of little more than half an hour.

"THE DEAD MUST NOT ARISE."

Makaba was another powerful chief with whom Mr. Moffat came in contact. His tribe was cleaner and, in some respects, more civilized than many others; and he himself was feared by all the surrounding tribes. It was Makaba's great desire to be on friendly terms with the white people; and he, therefore, cordially received Mr. Moffat on a visit which he paid him. The latter was most anxious to converse both with him and his people on divine things; but what he said on these subjects was received with indifference. One Sunday morning, determined to obtain a hearing, he went with some of his party into the town, and, sitting down beside Makaba, stated that his object was to tell him his news. Thinking to hear of some feats of war, the great man's countenance lighted up; but when he found that the news concerned the Saviour, of whom the day before he had confessed that he knew nothing, he resumed his knife and a jackal's skin, which he was cutting for the purpose of making a cloak, and hummed a native air. One of his men, however, seemed struck with the Redeemer's character, and with the account of his miracles. On hearing that he raised the dead, the man exclaimed, "What an excellent doctor he must have been, to make dead men live!" This led Mr. Moffat to speak of the general resurrection, when the chief caught the startling sound, and cried out, "What are these words about? The dead, the dead arise!" "Yes," was the reply; "all the dead shall arise." "Will my father arise?" "Yes, your father will arise." "Will all the dead slain in battle, and all that have been devoured by lions, tigers, hyenas, and crocodiles, again revive?" "Yes, and all come to judgment." "And will those whose bodies have been scattered to the winds again arise?" he asked, with a kind of triumph, as if he had now fixed him. "Yes," said the missionary, with increased emphasis, "not one will be left behind."

Turning to his people, Makaba asked if even the wisest of them ever heard such news, saying that he had supposed that he possessed all the knowledge of the country. At length he turned again, and, addressing Mr. Moffat, said, "Father, I love you much. Your visit and your presence have made my heart white as milk. The words of your mouth are sweet as honey ; but the words of a resurrection are too great to be heard. I do not wish to hear again about the dead rising! The dead cannot arise! The dead must not arise!" "Why," was the inquiry, "can so great a man refuse knowledge, and turn away from wisdom?" Raising and uncovering his arm, which had been strong in battle, and shaking his hand as if quivering a spear, he replied, "I have slain my thousands, and shall they arise?"

A CHRISTIAN'S SORROW FOR HEATHEN RELATIVES.

Mr. Moffat did not labour in vain. Among others, Mamonyatsi, a Matabele captive, who remained for some time in Mrs. Moffat's service, was an instance of the power of the gospel. She had early shown great readiness in learning to read, and much quickness of understanding. And from the time when first received into the church, to the day of her death, she was a living epistle easily known and read. After her marriage, while he was visiting the sick of his flock, Mr. Moffat one day entered her dwelling. He found her sitting and weeping, with a portion of God's word in her hand. "My child, what is the cause of your sorrow?" said he. "Is the baby still unwell?" "No," she replied, "my baby is well." "Your mother-in-law?" he continued. "No, no," she said; "it is my own dear mother who bore me." Here she gave vent to her grief, and holding out the Gospel of Luke, in a hand wet with tears, she said, "My mother will never see this Word; she will never hear this good news?" She wept again, and said, "Ah! my mother and my friends; they live in heathen darkness; and shall they die without seeing the light which has shone on me, and without tasting that love which I have tasted? My mother, my mother!"

AN AGED SINNER CONVERTED.

There was an old grandmother, who had wallowed in the very sewers of heathenism, and been an active agent of the wicked one in opposing the progress of the gospel. She hated the very sight of the places of Christian worship, and had taught many to blaspheme. One day, she entered the chapel in quest of a child, and was constrained to sit a few minutes. She had not heard many sentences, when she fled from the hated spot. On the Sabbath following she came again, when all who saw her felt alarmed, lest violence was intended against some one; but she quietly heard the voice of mercy, and retired in an orderly way. In the course of a few days, she went to Mr. Moffat in a state bordering on distraction. "My sins! my sins!" was her language, while tears streamed down her furrowed cheeks. Her half-frantic soul would hear no comfort, nor listen to any counsel. Night after night she would call him out of bed, to tell her what was to become of her soul. One day, when he met her in the street, she grasped his hands with both hers, exclaiming, "To live I cannot! I cannot die!" Again she was directed to the Lamb of God, and the fountain opened for her sins; but she interrupted by saying, "You say the blood of Christ cleanses from all sins; do you know the number of mine? Look to yonder grassy plain, and count the blades of grass, or the drops of dew; these are nothing to the amount of my transgressions." After continuing in this state several weeks, she was enabled to believe, when the being, who once persecuted and cursed all who bore the Christian name, was found sitting at the feet of Jesus, clothed, and in her right mind, adoring the riches of Divine grace to one who was, as she would describe herself, "like the mire of the streets."

A KAFFIR CHURCH.

"The dwellings of the Kaffirs are arranged in four parallel rows, and a fifth row is just begun. Between the houses of the people and ours stands the little chapel, also a round hut. The old chapel, which was erected shortly after the storm, only as a temporary building, was constructed of planks. These had lately become very loose; and it was scarcely fit for use. At the first conference after our arrival at Baziya, we resolved to ask permission to build a new chapel, which could serve as a school-room when we are able to erect a substantial and commodious place of worship. Permission being granted, we set to work at once. Our people were very glad when they were told what was intended, and expressed their willingness to aid as much as they could. It was very cheering to see how they hastened to the work when the signal was given; this I always gave by sounding the horn. They seemed to like this way of calling them together very much; and sometimes a number of them would stand round me, listening to every sound, and then would exclaim, '*mnandi! mnandi!*'—sweet! or beautiful! They laboured very hard; and although it was just the time to sow their millet-fields, they were nearly every day at work. On the 5th of December last, we planted the first pole in the ground, and on the 8th of January, this year, we were able to preach for the first time in the new house of God. All the work was done by our men gratuitously. It is really a nice strong hut, but twenty-seven feet in diameter, and with walls nearly eight feet high. The poles in the middle measure sixteen feet. There are two windows, of six panes each, and two or three panes. Our men are quite proud that they have built such a house." In this station of the Moravian missions there are being prepared, we trust, some of those lively stones which are to form part of the great spiritual temple, which is the church of the living God. One aged bushman, who was dull and slow of comprehension, desired to be a professed disciple of the Lord Jesus. He said, "I cannot tell how it comes, but I know I am very different from what I was."

A KAFFIR PREACHER.

"He had a noble audience. The church was crowded in every part by a most picturesque assembly of red-painted Kaffirs. To his left sat the men in their red blankets; to his right were the women, in full dress, with their skin karosses on, whilst their heads were decorated with such numerous and varied-coloured ornaments as would baffle the most skilful pen to describe. It was such a discourse as only Tiyo Soga can preach to these sable countrymen of his. He spoke to us of the name that shall endure forever; and we listened with bated breath to his eloquent appeals. The only fault of his sermon was its brevity. The two chiefs of the tribe were present, besides many petty chiefs. Oba was heard to say, 'There is something in what we have heard just now. Buy European clothes, and enter these churches, and listen to what these teachers say, and never say again that we, your chiefs, stand in the way of your embracing the gospel.' Kaka, an old chief, a thoroughly hardened sinner, said, as he walked out of the church, 'What is this? The son of Soga has brought a dimness across our eyes to-day, and we are quite unmanned.' Another said, 'If these words do not awaken us, I pronounce ourselves the most incorrigible of people.' I never knew that Soga was such an orator. This sermon was delivered at the opening of a new church in Henderson, Kaffraria."

THE GOSPEL REJECTED.

A missionary in South Africa says, "We once met a company of men, young and old, one of whom addressed us, as speaker for all, in the following language: 'Teacher, white man! we black people do not like the news you bring us. We are black; and we like to live in darkness. You trouble us; you break up our kraals, and eat up our cattle; you will be the ruin of our tribe. And now we tell you, to-day, if you do not cease, we will leave you and all this region, and go where the gospel is not known or heard.' 'But,' said I, 'how is this? If I oppose your customs, it is because the Word of God is opposed to them, and because they are wrong. Your children I teach, as I do you, to become wise, and good, and happy. But how do I eat up your cattle, and break up your kraals and your tribes? All that I obtain from you I pay for, do I not? And I sometimes try to do you a good turn besides.' 'Yes; but you teach repentance, and faith; and a penitent, believing man is to us as good as dead. He no longer takes pleasure in our pursuits, nor labours to build his father's kraal, but leaves it, and joins the church, and tries to lead others after him. And as to our cattle, our girls and our women are our cattle; but you teach that they are not cattle, and ought not to be sold for cattle, but to be taught, and clothed, and made the servants of God, and not the slaves of men. This is the way you eat up our cattle."

GOOD NEWS FROM SOUTH-EAST AFRICA.

After twelve years' efforts among the Wanika, our missionaries (Church Missionary Society) were compelled to leave the station, and retire, one to Zanzibar, there to engage himself in the study of languages, the other to Bombay. The result of their labours, after twelve years, seemed to be small indeed. Two converts, one of whom had been transferred to heaven, were all that they had gained.

But when the missionaries had left the coast, the Lord gave the word, and the seed sprang up. In June, 1859, the missionary Rebmann proceeded from Zanzibar on a short visit to the old sphere of labour,—the Wanika country; and, instead of meeting with the customary indifference, the people warmly welcomed him, saying, joyfully, "You have done well to come back to us." This decided him, the political circumstances which compelled him to leave having been removed, to resume his labours among this people.

He learned that, after the departure of the missionaries, the people had suffered much from the invasion of a wild tribe called the Wasai, from the interior. In this state they were found by Abbe Gunga, the Wanika convert, who, after accompanying Mr. Rebmann to Zanzibar, had returned home; nor had the chastisement to which they had been subjected been without effect. One man was first brought to think. His name was Mua Muamba, "the man of the rock;" and such he proved to be. Resolving to turn to the living God, he cast away his idols—the charms he had been making for guarding the plantations—to the moles and to the bats, and decided to go with Abbe Gunga to Zanzibar to see the missionary. During their absence other seed sprang up, and, on their return, three new converts were waiting to join them. Mua Muamba has since entered into his rest, being the second Mnika gathered in to join the great multitude of all tribes and nations before the throne. As if he had a presage of his early death, he had long before given injunctions to his wife and family that there should be no heathen ceremonies, either before or after his burial, and that instead of sitting together in idleness a whole week, as the old custom was, they should take up their hoes and cultivate the ground. His hut was situated about a mile distant from the mission station; and he and Abbe Gunga were among the most regular in their attendance on the Lord's day for prayer and instruction. His illness was short, not more than ten days, during which he was frequently visited. "His countenance was most happy when I spoke to him, one day, of Stephen, and the sufferings of the first Christians," writes Mr. Rebmann. "On the evening of January 30th, I again went to take him some medicine, and arrived at his hut just at sunset; when, to my great surprise and grief, I found he had just expired. His head was still placed on the lap of his wife, who, with tears in her eyes, told me that he had that morning, as usual, knelt at his bedside for prayer." His burial took place on the anniversary of the terrible invasion of the Wasai; and on that day "Christianity celebrated its first public victory over heathenism in East Africa," for instead of the horrible drumming and dancing, and the hellish sounds of lamentation and mirth mixed together, amidst which heathen Mnika are carried to the grave, the sounds which were heard over the grave of Mua Muamba, "the man of the rock," were those of the word of God.

The young people had made preparations indeed for the customary ceremonies; but they yielded to the persuasions of the missionary. Nor is it only among the people near the station that hopeful symptoms are found, but among those at a distance too. They are ready to confess that heathenism is at once a falsehood and a plague, from which they can only be delivered by "entering the book;" and they say, "We shall all lay hold on the book."

THE COMMENCEMENT OF THE MISSIONS IN MADAGASCAR.

The gospel was first carried to Madagascar in 1818, by some missionaries of the London Missionary Society. The king, Radama I., protected and encouraged them on account of the secular advantages which he saw that his country would derive from their instructions: schools were established, the Bible translated; and thus a certain amount of progress made, when in 1828 Radama died. He was succeeded by the eldest of his twelve wives, who usurped the throne, and, after a few years, determined to put a stop to the good work that was begun.

The missionaries were obliged to leave the island, and a dreadful persecution of the Christians began, which lasted until the death of the queen in 1861.

But the work was of God, and it was not his will that it should die out. A native ministry was raised up, without pressure from those who had been their teachers; and, besides this, the written word was so wonderfully blessed, that when, on the accession of Radama II., the island was once more open to the heralds of the gospel, the converts who came forth from their hiding-places were numbered by thousands.

THE MIDNIGHT MEETING.

It is midnight. The silence and darkness are unbroken. No voice nor footstep is heard in the streets of the capital. But here and there, individuals might have been discerned silently stealing along under the deep shadow of the houses. All these are bending their steps towards one point, the house of prayer. A smile of recognition, tempered with a shade of sadness and anxiety, glances from face to face as they enter. They join in prayer; but in the midst of their devotions a stranger enters. He is an officer of high rank in the army, an honourable and friendly man, but not hitherto known as a

Christian. Filled with surprise, not unmixed with apprehension, the brethren suspend the service, and wait in silence for an explanation. This is frankly given. The officer declares himself to be one of their number, and adds, that he had been constrained to join them in this their hour of weakness and peril, because he abhorred the injustice with which they had been treated by the queen. That was a memorable night in the history of these Christians. He who thus, when others shrunk away, came bravely forth to share their perils, proved subsequently one of their wisest counsellors and best protectors. Soon his wife followed his example, and she, with her husband, succoured very many.

THE PROTO-MARTYR.

Rasalama was the proto-martyr of Madagascar. During her imprisonment, it was reported to the judges that she had said, "When the Tsitialaingia came to my house I was not afraid, but rather rejoiced that I was counted worthy to suffer affliction for believing in Jesus," on which she was ordered to be put into heavy irons, and severely beaten; but throughout these sufferings, so long as she had strength, she sought comfort in singing her favourite hymns. During the afternoon preceding the day of her execution, the chains which she wore were exchanged for others, consisting of rings and bars fastened around her hands, feet, knees, and neck, which were then drawn together, and thus the whole body was forced into a position which caused great agony. Joyful, therefore, was the patient sufferer as the time drew on when death would release her from the tyrant's power.

As she was conducted to the place of execution, she continued to sing; and thus set an example which was followed by many who were afterwards called to tread the same pathway to death and heaven. Though many sympathized with Rasalama, and earnest prayers were offered on her behalf by Christian friends, yet they knew that by identifying themselves with her they would imperil their own lives. But there was one young man whom even this danger did not deter. Fearless of consequences, Rafarahahy pressed through the guard of soldiers, and walking as near to her side as he could, he said to her, "My sister, I will not leave you till the end." At length the gloomy procession reached the spot where this Christian woman was to suffer. The name of it is Ambohipotsy. It forms the southern extremity of the crest of the hill upon which the city stands. Though reviled by the heathen, she rested upon the Saviour, and reviled not again. The only request she made to her executioners was for a brief interval that she might pray. This was granted; and she kneeled down upon the rocky ground. Some said, "Where is the God she prays to, that he does not save her now?" Others looked on with pity. But she, regardless of all around, held communion with the divine Saviour; and while thus commending her spirit into his hands, the executioners from behind buried their spears in her body. So calm, so firm was this noble sufferer, that even the hard men who took her life were constrained to say, "There is some charm in the religion of the white people which takes away the fear of death;" while that courageous friend who had accompanied her to the last exclaimed, as he turned away from a spectacle at once so sorrowful and so sublime, "If I might die so tranquil and happy a death, I would not be unwilling to die for the Saviour too." This young man was eventually called in like manner, and at the same spot, to seal his faith with his blood.

PENALTIES FOR THE PROFESSION OF CHRISTIANITY.

One Christian wrote, "I was condemned to slavery, and valued at thirty dollars. My wife and children also were made slaves. My property was all taken from me. I was aide-de-camp to Rainiharo, and had been promoted to the eighth honour (about equal to an English colonelcy). But mine honour was taken from me, and I was made a common soldier, to carry a musket, and perform the exercise of a soldier once a fortnight, until my skin peeled off like that of a serpent, every time we performed the exercise; for we were not allowed to wear eather a hat or a shirt, but only a girdle round our loins. 'Blessed be God who lightens our sorrows.' (2 Cor. v.)"

TWO GREAT EXECUTIONS.

Nineteen Christians lay under sentence of death; and at one o'clock, on the morning previous to their execution, individuals and groups might have been seen quietly leaving their dwellings and stealing noiselessly along the streets. The word had passed from lip to lip that they were to meet and pray for their suffering brethren. The voice of strong crying and prayer had scarcely died away, and the morning light had not yet appeared, when the city was all astir. Swiftly and widely had the intelligence spread on the previous evening that the decree of the queen had gone forth; and great multitudes now hastened to the spots where these noble martyrs were to demonstrate the sincerity of their faith in Jesus. There were two spots to be rendered almost sacred by the sufferings and the spirit of those who were there cruelly sacrificed upon that day. One is called Arapimarinana, or "the place of hurling down." It is in the midst of the city; and the place of execution is a precipice of granite one hundred and fifty feet high, over which condemned persons were flung. And hither on that dreadful morning pressed the gathering throng. But let us turn from them to the prison. Meek, like their divine Master, though seized with rude violence and flung upon the ground, no complaint escapes the sufferers' lips. As they sat upon the ground, with heart and voice they unite in singing a favourite hymn, which thus begins:—

"When I shall die and leave my friends,
When they shall weep for me,
When departed has my life,
Then I shall happy be!"

Martyrdom of Native Christians at Madagascar. p. 174.

And when that hymn was ended, they began another, the first line of which is,—

> "When I shall, rejoicing, behold Him in the heavens."

But these sounds of sacred melody were now drowned by the hoarse, harsh voice of the queen's messenger, who, in the name of Ranavalona, is pronouncing upon each the sentence they were that day to suffer. Four of them were nobles, two of whom were husband and wife. As it was unlawful to shed the blood of persons of their rank, they were to be burned alive, and the remaining fifteen to be thrown from the place of hurling down. As the officer was leaving the prison, the nobles sent a request to the queen that they might be strangled before their bodies were burned: but that mercy was denied them. The fifteen wrapped in mats, and with mats thrust into their mouths, to prevent them speaking to each other or to the people, were then hung by their hands and feet to poles, and carried to the place of execution. But the attempt wholly to stop their mouths failed; for they prayed, and addressed the crowd as they were borne along. "And some," we are told, "who beheld them, said that their faces were like the faces of angels."

Thus they reached Arapimarinana. A rope

was then firmly tied round the body of each, and, one by one, fourteen of them were lowered a little way over the precipice. Then, for the last time, the question was addressed to them, "Will you cease to pray?" But the only answer returned was an emphatic "No." Upon this, the signal was given, the rope was cut, and in another moment the mangled and bleeding body lay upon the rocks below. One of these brave sufferers for Christ, whose name was Ramonambonina, as he was led to the edge of the precipice, begged his executioners to give him a short time to pray, "for on that account," he said, "I am to be killed." His request being granted, he kneeled down, and prayed very earnestly; and, having risen from his knees, he addressed the people with such powerful and subduing eloquence, that all were amazed, and many struck with awe. Then, turning to his executioners, he said, "My body you will cast down this precipice, but my soul you cannot, as it will go up to heaven to God; therefore, it is gratifying to me to die in the service of my Maker."

One severe part of the fiery trial through which these Christians passed on to their rest with God was their being placed where they could see the fall of their brethren, and then asked whether they would recant. But they seemed so filled with the love of their Saviour, and with the joyful hope of heaven, that they utterly despised all offers of life on such conditions. One of them, a beautiful and accomplished young woman, a favourite with the queen, who wished to save her, thus refused, and manifested so much determination to go with her brethren and sisters to heaven, that the officer standing by said, "You are a fool! You are mad!" And then sent to the queen, saying that she had lost her reason, and should be sent to some place of safe keeping. She thus escaped, and afterwards was married to a Christian man, and died only a few years ago.

Meanwhile, the other martyrs walked calmly to where the stakes had been fixed in the ground, singing as they went. "At the moment when they were brought to the stakes," writes an eye-witness, "a remarkable phenomenon occurred. A rainbow, of an immense size, and forming a triple arch, stretched across the heavens. One end of it appeared to the spectators to rest on the posts to which the martyrs were tied. The rain, meanwhile, fell in torrents, and the multitudes who were present were so struck with amazement and terror at the occurrence, that many of them took to flight." The pile was kindled, and then, from amidst the crackling and roaring of the fire, were heard, not the sounds of pain, but the song of praise. That scene, and the hymn which the martyrs sang, as they rose in their fiery chariot to heaven, will never be forgotten in Madagascar. But prayer followed praise. "O Lord," they were heard to cry, "receive our spirits; for thy love to us has caused this to come to us; and lay not this sin to their charge!"

"Thus," says a witness of the memorable scene, "they prayed as long as they had any life. Then they died; but softly, gently. Indeed, gently was the going forth of their life, and astonished were all the people around that beheld the burning of them there."

THIRSTING FOR GOD'S WORD.

Afflicted, destitute, and tormented, wandering in the forests, or sold into a cruel slavery, these poor Christians of Madagascar clung to their Bibles with a wonderful affection. The queen's command, enforced by dreadful threats, that all books should be delivered up, was disobeyed by many. A few Bibles were saved at great risk by their possessors; but these were so diligently read, and so often lent, that they were almost worn out, and the letters received by friends in Mauritius and in England were filled with pressing requests for a new supply of the sacred treasure. "Exceedingly afflicted are we," they wrote, "on account of the fewness of the Bibles here with us; and we exceedingly desire to have more. We are thirsting for them; for the Bible is our companion and friend to instruct, and search in thoroughly, when in secrecy and silence, and to comfort us in our grief and tribulation. Send us many, for even then they will not be enough, and let them be in small print so as to be easily hidden. As to the condition of the country, it is still dark, and there is still persecution by the queen. Nevertheless, the people are going forward. Blessed be God who thus prospers them!" And the writers added that many of the men travelled a long distance to some secluded hill or valley every Saturday; so, he said, as to get beyond the reach of the people, that none may see us, and that we may spend the Sabbath together in worshipping God. But the women are not strong enough to walk so far, and this makes us feel very much on account of the sorrow of those who cannot go.

A LONG JOURNEY FOR A BIBLE.

When Mr. Ellis was at Mauritius, he received a letter from a Christian, who had nearly lost his sight in consequence of having devoted years in copying portions of Scripture for his brethren. And one evening, while he was at Tamatave, on the eastern coast of Madagascar, two men called at the house where he was staying. They had heard that he had brought the Bible to their land, and had travelled a long distance to get a copy. Fearing, however, that they might be spies, he put them off until the next day, in order that he might make inquiries about them. But some Christians of the place knew them to be excellent men, who had travelled more than a hundred miles in order to secure the sacred treasure. Of course, he was delighted to receive them the next day, and to give them what they wanted. But before doing so, he entered into conversation with them, and found that they were members of a large and scattered family, and that all were Christians. They had seen the Scriptures, and heard them, they said, and also themselves as a family possessed "some of the words of David," which they were in the habit of passing on from one to another. He then inquired whether they had these "words of David" with them? This was a question which they seemed unwilling to answer; but at length they confessed that they had. Mr. Ellis having requested to see the book, they looked at one another, and appeared as if they knew not what to do. At length one of them thrust his hand deep into his bosom, and from beneath the folds of his lamba drew forth a parcel. This he very slowly and carefully opened. One piece of cloth after another having been gently unrolled, at length there appeared a few leaves of the book of Psalms, which the good man cautiously handed to Mr. Ellis. Though it was evident that the greatest care had been taken of them, their soiled appearance, worn edges, and other marks of frequent use, showed plainly enough how much they had been read.

Desiring to possess these precious fragments, Mr. Ellis asked the men whether they had not seen other words of David besides those which they now produced, and also the words of Jesus and of Paul, of Peter and of John? Yes, they replied; they had seen them and heard some of them, but did not possess them. "Well, then," said Mr. Ellis, holding out the tattered leaves, "if you will give me these few words of David, I will give you all his words, and I will give you, besides, the words of Jesus, and of John, and of Paul, and of Peter." Upon this he handed to them a copy of the New Testament and the Psalms bound together, and said, "You shall have all these if you will give me this."

The men were at first amazed. Then they compared the Psalms they had with those in the book, and having satisfied themselves that all their own words of David were in it, with many more, and that besides these there were other Scriptures which they greatly desired, light beamed in their faces; they took Mr. Ellis at his word, gave him those leaves of the book of Psalms which had so long yielded them comfort, seized the volume he offered in exchange, bade him farewell, and hastily left the house. In the course of the day he inquired after them, wishing to speak to them again, when the Christians at Tamatave told him that as soon as they left the house they set out upon their long journey homewards, "rejoicing as one that findeth great spoil."

"Tell all the Christians in your country that we are famishing and hungering for the bread of life. Contrive deep schemes to send us Bibles; for we are as a hundred to one plate at this time, because the books that were formerly received from you have all been burnt."

THE MORNING OF JOY.

It was in 1861 that the night of weeping in Madagascar was brought to a close by the death of the bloodthirsty queen Ranavalona; and her son Radama II., who had long been a friend to the Christians, ascended the throne, to the great joy of the whole nation; for many who were not Christians themselves sympathized with them in their sufferings. Then did the exiles hasten home, and men and women, worn with suffering and want, reappeared in the city, to the astonishment of their neighbours, who had long believed them to be dead. The London Missionary Society hastened to reoccupy the ground; and Mr. Ellis sailed on his fourth visit to Madagascar. On his arrival a house was appropriated to his use by the king, and officers were sent to conduct him to it. The day after his arrival was the Sabbath; but to him it was not a day of rest. At an early hour his house was invaded by Christian friends, and from nine o'clock until two he was led from one congregation to another, that he might, though in an unknown tongue and through an interpreter, utter some words of prayer to God, and exhortations to the people. During that morning he took part in five services. "Wherever I went," he said, "I was saluted with tears and expressions of joy; and whenever I pronounced the blessed name of Jesus Christ, it was truly affecting to witness the utterance of deep emotion by which they testified their faith and gratitude."

After spending a week at Tamatave, a special messenger from the king arrived to hasten his departure for the capital. When within thirty miles of it he was met by a large number of Christians from the city, headed by two pastors; but instead of expressing their joy by ordinary salutations, they came towards him with the voice of thanksgiving and melody. Tears, he tells us, were the only response which he could make to the devout gladness of his friends. This real *Te Deum* ended, the pastors announced that they had been sent by their brethren and the churches to bid him welcome. During the week Mr. Ellis's house was thronged, and the only drawback to the people's joy seemed to be that he had not been able to bring with him copies of God's word. This was not surprising, as some whole congregations did not possess a single copy. Nevertheless, he found their faith simple, scriptural, and firm; and religion seemed to be with them a real, sincere, earnest, personal concern.

HEATHEN MALAGASY.

The island of Madagascar is nine hundred miles in length; and, notwithstanding the wonders which God has wrought in it, there are many districts still entirely heathen, and in

Malagese Chiefs and Native Woman. p. 184.

which the gospel has never been preached. Since the death of the cruel Ranavalona, other societies, besides the one which had the honour of first entering this noble field, have stepped in, and are labouring in some of these untouched provinces. The Rev. T. Campbell, of the Church Missionary Society, thus describes some of the Malagasy who were still in their unconverted state:—

"During my stay in Tamatave, I visited and conversed with many of the people, who seemed to be much given to the practice of drinking. In this the Betsimisarakas appear to outstrip the Sakalavas of the north. In many of the houses a barrel of rum is to be seen; and in the evenings these houses are filled with people shouting, singing, and drinking."

Again he writes:—"On Saturday morning, early, I retraced my stepts to Andavoranto, and had not been on the road many hours when we came to a small village, which was all in an uproar. Inquiring the cause, we were told that a man had stolen a child, and carried it off to sell as a slave. Several men went into the forest in search of the thief, one of whom had a spear in his hand. They may, or may not, succeed in finding the child, which may be hopelessly sold into slavery. This stealing of children is, I am told, not uncommon here, and is one of the great evils of domestic slavery in this country; in fact, there is nothing but slavery here; no one can think or act independently. The great people are the slaves of the Government, and the poor are the slaves of the great, and these slaves, in turn, possess slaves. Nothing but the gospel of Jesus Christ can make them free in every respect, and in the highest sense of the term; but "if the truth shall make them free, then they shall be free indeed."

OF ONE MIND.

The Gospel Propagation Society has stations in the neighbourhood of Tamatave, and Mr. Hey, one of their missionaries, proposed to Mr. Campbell to accompany him on a visit to some of these on the sea-coast lying to the north of that town. At Mahavelona they held two services, and after the second, going out to visit the people, and the houses in which the congregation connected with the London Missionary Society met being pointed out to them, they entered it, and found it well filled with men and women. "The leaders of the congregation made way for us," says Mr. Campbell, "and accommodated us with seats." We asked if prayers were over, and being answered in the negative, we expressed our willingness to join with them. We were at once asked to take the service; and at their and Mr. Hey's request, I took it. I gave out a hymn, and then asked the chief man to pray. After this I preached from Matthew v. 13-16. The congregation was most attentive throughout. I then gave out another hymn, and asked the second in command to offer up prayer, which he did in a quiet, earnest manner. We then sang "Lord, dismiss us with thy blessing," and departed, receiving several warm shakes of the hand as we left.

OPENING OF THE SECOND MEMORIAL CHURCH.

At an early hour large crowds of the natives, dressed in clean, snow-white lambas, squatted themselves beneath the plantains, awaiting the arrival of the sovereign,—it being Malagasy "jomba" that the queen must enter the new building first. The procession, headed by a military band, with the Maranitra, or Queen's Guards, as a guard of honour, left the palace at about eight o'clock. As the queen passed the Roman Catholic Chapel the priests paid "hasina" (a dollar of allegiance). When the procession reached the clear space, the *tout ensemble*, as seen from the high ground near the southernmost cannon, must have been very pleasing, the queen's scarlet umbrella being a prominent object. The members of the Mission, with Dr. Davidson and the friends, received the queen at the tower entrance, the queen shaking hands with all of us. It being law that no one must sit higher than the queen, I had the floor in the eastern transept gallery raised for her accommodation, and also for the prime minister. As soon as the queen had taken her seat, those who were to lead the singing were admitted at the vestry door. When these were seated, the prime minister ordered the doors to be opened, and the building was speedily filled in every part. Mr. Toy had taken great pains to train the singers, numbering about two hundred; they had met in the house of one of the most influential members of the Government eight successive mornings (Sunday excepted) at seven o'clock for practice, and the "service of song," which included three anthems, was very acceptably rendered, the tunes being those we have been accustomed to join in in "our own dear land." The harmonium used was that sent out for the Andohalo Church; and I think the benevolent donor would have been well pleased had he realized the service the instrument rendered on that day. Pardon my saying that the congregation would have purchased a similar instrument, having four rows of vibrators and swell, were not the necessity laid on them to build a new school-room immediately; they will, however, gladly bear the expense of its transit up the country, should any English friend be disposed to present one to this church. When quiet was obtained, the Malagasy National Anthem re-arranged was sung to appropriate words, which Mr. Toy had prepared. The prime minister then rose and paid "hasina" for the congregation. This necessitated a short speech, in which he urged the people to trust in Christ as their only Saviour, etc. Mr. Toy, the minister of the church, then read a statement, setting forth the purpose for which the memorial churches are being erected, and the service was proceeded with in the usual manner, excepting that besides an exposition of church principles, there were two sermons, the one by a native preacher, the other by a missionary. I leave the report of the meeting to Mr. Toy, who will, doubtless, give more definite particulars than I can be expected to do, simply adding that we are grateful for the bold, outspoken exhibition of the truth listened to on that day, as well as the admirable manner in which it was delivered. It has been much spoken of by the natives.

NORTH AMERICA AND THE WEST INDIES.

ELIOT, THE APOSTLE OF THE NORTH AMERICAN INDIANS.

It was in 1646 that John Eliot, an exile from England for the gospel's sake, became Christ's messenger to the poor scattered Indians in Massachusetts, Rhode Island, and Connecticut. For some years he had been the pastor of an infant church near Boston, and during this time he had mastered the language of these poor lost sheep. At length, accompanied by three friends, he took a journey to the first Indian settlement; and no missionary ever had a more encouraging reception. Headed by their chief, Waubon, the natives gathered round him to learn what the white man had to say. With his Bible in his hand, Eliot at once knelt down and earnestly besought his Master's blessing on the message which he was about to deliver,—the Indians keeping perfect silence during this prayer, as well as during the hour's address which followed. Waubon was his firm friend from that day; for the word was not only at once received with joy, but it made a lasting impression. Day after day, meetings were held for the instruction of the people; and at the third of these the chief himself took part, and spoke of the things which he had heard with wild and fervid eloquence. After this, other chiefs came forward and desired instruction for their subjects, while the children were willingly given up for Christian instruction. It was clear that Eliot had come to a people prepared of the Lord; but such success was unexpected, and he could but stand amazed at what God had done by him

For sixty years he continued to make these missionary journeys whenever his pastoral work at Boston permitted. Waubon became as a brother to him, and very early shared his work. It was a heavy grief to Eliot when he was summoned to his death-bed. He found it surrounded by chiefs and warriors, as well as by his own family; and the dying Indian chief was bidding them not to weep for him, and so passed away, with words of faith and hope on his lips.

Eliot's work was cheered and lightened by his wife, who was as a nursing-mother to the church; and thus he was enabled not only to preach, but to translate the Scriptures into the Indian tongue. He was blessed, also, in his five sons, who fully entered into their father's longings, though only two survived the age of early manhood. He himself lingered to the age of ninety, and had the happiness of seeing his numerous converts settled in fourteen places, which were called "praying stations."

HANS EGEDE, THE FIRST MISSIONARY TO GREENLAND; OR, SERVING IN FAITH.

Seven or eight hundred years ago, there were Icelandic and Norwegian colonies, and Christian churches in Greenland. Those colonies and churches have long since become utterly extinct; nevertheless, it was a tradition of their existence, related, among other tales, to a little boy, in Norway, named Hans Egede, which led to the commencement of the Greenland missions. He never forgot that story; and the desire to go and preach the gospel in that far-off land was for many years like a consuming fire within him. To his friends the project seemed wild and absurd; and for a long time obstacles innumerable stood in the way,—his wife's opposition being the greatest of all. But when she gave way,—said that she could renounce every thing for his sake, and, at length, having spread the matter before God in prayer, became even more anxious to go than she had been to stay,—his mind was made up; and it was not long before, under the protection of Christian IV., the husband and wife, with their four children, were conveyed to that country which is so unlike its name.

There, for fifteen long, dreary years, Hans Egede sowed the seed, of which he was never permitted to reap the fruit. Once a year only they were visited by a ship from Norway, bringing them letters and provisions; so it was a lonely work. But, by degrees, an influence was gained over the natives, so that he was permitted to instruct and baptize many children. But still it was in bitterness of soul that he pursued his course; for not one single convert was made during his ministry. His only hope, he said, was in his Father in heaven, and his only earthly comfort the fortitude and unshaken faith of his wife. Her face was always bright, and her spirit cheerful. At length she was taken from him; and, soon after, quite crushed, the weary labourer, at the request of his sovereign, returned to his native land, and devoted his remaining days to the one business of teaching the language, which he had acquired with so much labour, to the students of a college which was to furnish his successors.

THE PREACHING OF THE CROSS OF CHRIST.

Early in the eighteenth century the Moravian settlement of Herrnhut was formed in Upper Lusatia in the dominion of Lewis, Count Zinzendorf, who had granted this refuge to these poor, persecuted Christians at the request of a certain Christian David. Shortly after, this good man and the count both heard that the Greenland mission was to be abandoned by the Government; and of this, word was sent to the praying people of Herrnhut. This was before Hans Egede had left.

Christian David, and his cousin, Matthew Stach, on the first account of Greenland, felt a strong desire to go there, "hoping that the apostle of Greenland, Egede, could and would make use of them." They went to Copenhagen, but at first met only with discouragement. It was urged that if the learned and pious Egede had effected so little, it could not be expected that success would attend the labours of such illiterate men. But one nobleman about the court suggested to the king that weak instruments were often made use of to bring about God's designs in the world. His arguments were so effectual that the king not only gave his consent, but wrote with his own hand to Egede on their behalf. Some others went with them, it appears; for their accounts tell of five brethren who used, year by year, to meet together to witness the annual departure of the sun.

They also had to wait for success; and sometimes hope sank so low that the idea of returning home was discussed. Matthew Stach, however, could not be brought to think of it. He said, "At evening time it shall be light," a verse which had been impressed on his mind when he first began to think of the mission. And very soon after, when the five brethren were again assembled, and a few natives with them, the New Testament was opened, and the account of the crucifixion read. Then it was that the blessing descended. A man named

Kaiarnac rose up, stood in front of the reader, and in a loud, earnest voice said, "How was that? Tell me that once more, for I would fain be saved too." Joyfully, indeed, and yet with tears, was that request listened to, and the blessed tale of love once more repeated. He spoke, and the dew from above descended on many a heart; so that other eager listeners stood around, and the accents of prayer were heard from many a poor Greenlander. Now the good news spread quickly, for those who had received the truth proclaimed the Saviour to those around them. Along the coast, in the interior, and in the great market of the frozen Bay of Disco, with icebergs on every side, there sounded the song of praise and thanksgiving to God our Saviour.

The pious Egede had striven to make the people see their need of such a Saviour; but these simple-minded Moravians just told the old story of peace, and God blessed the telling of it.

FIRST MISSIONARIES TO LABRADOR.

It was in the last half of the eighteenth century that the Moravian Church sent its first missionaries to Labrador, Jans Haven and his young English wife. They had one companion for a time; but he soon pushed on northward, and the young couple remained to labour alone in this dreary land. With their own hands they built their house, and soon they might have been seen lying down to rest at night enveloped each in a bag of reindeer skin, while a little bag of the same kind lay beside them. The cold was so intense that the milk with which their babe was fed had to be cut with a hatchet before it was put to warm; and constantly, during the night, had they to rouse themselves to see if the infant breathed, and to keep the stove up to the heat necessary to maintain life.

It was a question at first how the natives would regard their visitors; but God gave them favour in their eyes; and very soon Jans and Mary had each their daily group of learners, while it became evident that their labour was not in vain. The young Englishwoman had left a sweet society of kindred spirits in order to teach these benighted women; but she had her reward when one and another of the Esquimaux became a sister in Christ; and it was among the women that the first drops of the heavenly shower fell. Ere long, however, Jans Haven found himself pastor of a little church of thirty-eight members of both sexes, while fifty others were under instruction.

ESQUIMAUX TEACHERS.

The Moravians have lately sent two Esquimaux from the missions in Labrador to preach the gospel to the more distant heathen, and they are spoken of as men who possess "a good knowledge of Scripture, a good flow of words, and a right humble opinion of themselves." One of them, Daniel, took with him a wife, four boys, and a sick infant, who died a few days later. The other, Gottlob, takes his wife and two children, one of them a poor crippled daughter, who will, probably, not live long, and who had to be carried on a stretcher to the boats. On the evening before they started, "a beautiful rainbow spread its arch over Daniel's boat in the bay, and Gottlob's tent on the shore, which the men regarded as a token of God's mercy, as it had been to Noah of old."

HARDSHIPS OF LABRADOR MISSIONS.

The Moravian missionaries in Labrador labour under every external disadvantage. In Zoar, one year their whole harvest consisted of a barrel of potatoes, about the size of walnuts, and a plentiful supply of radishes, all raised in a little garden made of sand mixed with earth brought from a more southern soil. In Hebron,

the garden-plot is at a great distance from the mission premises, as no sufficiently sheltered ground can be found near them; and, as it is, the garden must be kept constantly watered to prevent the gales from sweeping away the soil and its produce. In Umanak, Greenland, the missionaries have scraped off the turf over the pebbles, dried it, and rubbed it in their hands, and carried it in barrels to the garden-plot, where it is spread thinly over a layer of refuse bones, collected from before the doors of the Greenlanders' huts. Several years of such labour may, finally, accumulate a soil thick enough to dig up with a spade. The failure of a seal fishery, or of the ptarmigan hunt, reduces the missionaries and their docile flocks almost to a state of starvation.

HOW THE WORD OF GOD WAS FIRST CARRIED TO RUPERT'S LAND.

"I have trodden the burnt ruins of houses and farms, a mill, a fort, and sharpened stockades, but none of a place of worship, even on the smallest scale. I blush to say that, throughout the whole extent of the Hudson's Bay territories, no such building exists." These words were written by a governor of York Fort, in 1815, one hundred and forty-five years after the country was taken possession of by England! Five years later, however, the first step was taken towards wiping away this crying shame; and the Rev. John West was sent out to Red River station as a sort of missionary chaplain. Two young Indian boys were given to him on his journey through the country; they knew little of English and nothing of God; so his work began by teaching them. On his arrival at the station, he found between five and six hundred English and Scotch settlers, besides many half-breeds and Indians, all of whom were without any public means of grace. The children were uneducated; the parents, generally speaking, were unmarried, and the Sabbath utterly disregarded; and besides this settlement, Mr. West's sphere of labour reached three or four hundred miles into the interior; but, undaunted by discouragements and difficulties, he gave notice of divine service for the very day after his arrival, and was cheered by a crowded and attentive audience.

After remaining at this station for about three months, he started in January to visit two distant outposts, and find out the scattered Indians. He travelled in a sort of sledge, called a "cariole," drawn by dogs, and, under favourable circumstances, was sometimes carried by these faithful creatures a distance of about eighty miles in twenty-four hours. His route lay through immense plains of snow; and the only living creatures that occasionally broke the stillness of the scene were the buffaloès, which travelled in enormous herds, sometimes amounting to thousands, and the wolves that follow their track. At night, his attendants sought for a spot where there were plenty of trees, kindled a fire, and prepared the evening meal, after which they would spread their blankets on the frozen snow, and covering themselves with robes of buffalo skin, lie down to rest till morning. The thermometer stood sometimes at forty degrees below zero.

After about a month's absence he returned, and prepared to gather Indian children into a school,—a work which their wandering habits rendered very difficult. After a time, Mr. West returned to England to fetch his family, and circumstances prevented his return; but he had accomplished a great work in a short period; and when Mr. Jones, his successor, arrived, he found a very different state of things to that which had existed only three years before. A church had been built, schools established, the Sabbath was well observed, and the habits of the people much improved, while four of the

Indian scholars had been baptized; and, above all, some of the settlers were truly converted to God, while even in the hunting-grounds the power of the gospel was seen in the changed lives of many who were thus forced to be absent from the public means of grace.

TRIALS AND DIFFICULTIES OF THE FIRST MISSIONARIES.

Hudson's Bay is blocked up by fields of ice, except for a very short time during the summer; so that supplies from England can only reach the missionaries once a year. They were, therefore, obliged to clear and cultivate land, and rear cattle; and this not only to supply their own wants, for they were often surrounded by numbers of starving Indians and half-breeds who subsist entirely by hunting, and are so utterly improvident, that they never make provision for any time beyond the present. Mr. Jones's health also had been much injured by the severity of the first winter, so that he had broken a blood-vessel in the lungs; yet for two years he was alone in the mission, with Sunday and week-day services at two different places, the care of schools, pastoral visitation, and all this pressure of secular work, and not until October, 1825, was he joined by Mr. and Mrs.

Cochran. Their arrival was succeeded by some of the greatest troubles that the colony had ever known. The hunting expedition failed; and consequently a state of semi-starvation was endured by many of the poor people during the winter; and on the setting in of spring, the river being swollen by the melting of an unusual quantity of snow, it burst its icy bounds, and came rushing down into the settlement. With the thermometer still below freezing point, the inhabitants had to forsake their houses and flee, driving their cattle before them, on to the hills in different directions, and pitching their tents wherever they could, knowing that their houses and property were being carried away by the resistless flood. For a time the upper church and mission-house remained untouched, amid the general desolation. But gradually the waters rose, and the missionaries had to secure as much of their property as they could in the roof of the church. They also prepared a wooden platform in case of sudden necessity, and on one Sunday the service was held on this. At length the wind became so strong that this was no longer a place of safety. They had to procure boats, and follow the other colonists up to the hills, where for a whole month, they had to remain during the most inclement weather.

During one night all the tents and wigwams were blown down by a hurricane; and in the confusion a spark fell on the long grass, which was instantly in a flame, so that but for a heavy torrent of rain which extinguished the fire, they would all have perished.

Not until the middle of June could they return, and then only three houses, one of which was happily the mission-house, were found standing.

GATHERING IN THE HEATHEN.

There was a place called the "Grand Rapids," at about fifteen miles from the Upper Settlement; and here, as it was a place of resort for the Indians and half-breeds, Mr. Cochran erected for himself and family a log-house. He gained the confidence of the people by acting for them in almost every capacity in which they required a friend; but, as he had said, his work was no sinecure, for they were scattered over twelve miles of country, without roads, and full of swamps and creeks. Very soon his little congregation of thirty had increased to three hundred; for they came from all parts. "When," he said, "I speak to my own people of our state by nature, of a Saviour, of repentance and faith, and of the condition of the heathen, I sometimes stop, and put this thrilling question, 'Are not your relations in this state? Are they not heathen? Are not their bodies perishing for want of food, and their souls for lack of knowledge?' This often led them to think about their unfortunate relations in the wilderness, and they would tell their anxiety to some trusty friend going to York Fort, where men come from all parts of this vast continent; and so at last it reached the persons for whom it was intended; and often they would go up to the Grand Rapids to hear what this new thing could be."

One of these cases was that of a man, who, according to Indian fashion, had taken two sisters as his wives. He came and pitched his tent near that of a relation; and he and some other neighbours immediately began to speak to the new family about Christianity. Especially they pointed out the sinfulness of their present mode of life; and soon the women became so convinced of this, that one of them left her husband, and went to live in a separate tent. They constantly attended the service; but not until this poor woman became ill, did either of them send for Mr. Cochran to visit them. Then she told him, "When I came here, fifteen months ago, it was to hear about this new religion, and

I intended to accept it, if it proved as good as was reported. I came; I inquired; all was new, and astonished me. Oh! I thought, if I can but escape the bad place, and obtain the good one! I was told that I must put away my sins, and believe on Him who came into the world and died to save sinners. I considered; I felt willing to give up my Indian ways; as I came to the knowledge of bad things, I put them away, and I now go on putting them away."

THE BOY HELPERS.

In 1825, two sons of chiefs were sent by their fathers to the mission-school; and so satisfied was Mr. Jones with their conduct and progress, that before paying a visit to England, in 1828, he baptized them by the names of Kootamey and Spogan Garry. While Mr. Jones was away, these boys earnestly begged to be allowed to visit their own country. Mr. Cochran trembled for the results, but at length he allowed them to go; and in a few months they, to his great joy, returned, bringing with them five other boys of different tribes, who spoke languages so unlike that they could only communicate by signs.

Kootamey gave great promise of future usefulness; but he died in 1830, from the effects of a fall, leaving good grounds for hope that he had exchanged this life for a better.

Spogan Garry returned to his own people two years afterwards; and nothing was heard of him for four years, when Mr. Jones received, in a letter from a friend, the cheering news that he spent most of his time in instructing his people, in whom he had excited an anxious desire for further instruction, so that when any messengers arrived at the fort near to them, they would send and ask "if any new doctrines had arrived."

"ONLY PITY US."

A remarkable Indian movement has just taken place in British Columbia. A whole tribe of Indians asked the Rev. Mr. Good to visit them. They grew so impatient, that they telegraphed him at short intervals. For several days the feeling was intense. He taught them divine truth, of which they did not seem to weary. They then asked him to come and live with them, and be their father. He said, "If I come, I must find great fault with you, and make you put away many evil things which you now do." They said, "Only pity us, and come, and we will do what you tell us." Mr. Good has gone to be their pastor.

A CHIMSYAN INDIAN'S QUESTION.

All over that vast tract of country which is known as North-west America, there roam various tribes of red Indians. In their uncivilized state they wander about, and do not settle down in any particular places, because they live almost entirely by hunting; but they are naturally often attracted to European settlements formed by the great fur-trading companies, which are generally called forts, and some settle round them.

In the year 1856, it was decided that a mission should be begun at Fort Simpson, which is situated in a very northerly part of the Rocky Mountains; and Mr. Duncan, who had just gone through the Highbury Training College for Schoolmasters, willingly started, at a few days' notice, for this distant sphere of labour. Nine months afterwards he had reached his post, and was collecting Chimsyan sentences. The poor Indians were soon made to understand why he had come; and they took a great deal of interest in his study of their language. He found a young Indian who was willing to act as interpreter, and before he was able to speak much of the Chimsyan language himself, they started together to visit the Indian camp. The houses were large and strong, and they entered one hundred and forty of them, and saw cluster after cluster of half-naked, painted savages seated round their fires. But everywhere Mr. Duncan was greeted with "Claw-how-yah," a complimentary term used in the trading jargon. Then there was a general movement, and squattings, followed by a breathless silence, during which every eye was fixed on him; and then several would begin nodding and smiling, and saying, in a loud tone, "Ahm—ahm-at-met—ahm shimanget;" that is, "Good—good person—good chief."

In some houses he was treated with such honour, that he was seated on a box covered with a mat; for he was regarded as a person who had come to put them in possession of that great secret about eternal things which they believed that the whites had in their keeping. A dim notion of a supreme Being and a future state, with a tradition about the flood, was all the religion they possessed; and their dark religious rites, which were performed by medicine-men, only filled their minds with terror; but they were longing for instruction.

"What do mean by saying the year 1858?" asked Mr. Duncan's Indian interpreter, one day; and the question brought the awful fact vividly before his mind, that for all that time the blessed gospel had been in the world, and yet these poor creatures were still living in a darkness that might be felt. "What have Christians in ages gone by been thinking about, and what are they doing even at present?" he exclaimed.

A FRUITFUL TEN YEARS.

"I feel like an infant, not able to say much; but I know that my heart is turned to God, and that he has given his Son to wash away my sins in his blood.

"My sins have stood in my way; I wish to put them off. I believe in Jesus."

These were the baptismal confessions of two aged candidates out of ninety-six baptized by the Dean of Victoria, ten years after Mr. Duncan's arrival. There was then a congregation of four hundred, who might be seen every Sunday, streaming in two lines towards the church in the centre of the village, all dressed in their best attire.

THE PIPE OF PEACE.

The Rev. Henry Budd, a native minister, started in the winter of 1853–4, as missionaries in Rupert's Land are wont to do in the winter season, Indian hunting. For a long distance his course lay through a wide plain,—no woods to be seen, and no living creature but wolves and foxes playing around. The snow, however, was heaped up here and there by the nose of the buffalo, and carcases of those creatures were seen lying in every direction,—the Indians having left them to be devoured by wolves and crows. At length they reached the tent of the old man who was head of the tribe of which they were in search. He received them cordially, and bid his wife put on the kettle. She soon had ready a dish of fresh meat and buffalo tongues. A large family of children and grandchildren lived with the old man in his tent, and soon other Indians came flocking in. The old man was busy getting his tobacco-box full of cut tobacco and smoking-weed mixed, and filling his pipe of peace. At length the large pipe was lighted, and the stem pointed to the four quarters of the world. Then it was given to the oldest son, who gave it two or three sucks, and then handed it to another next to him; and so on, till the pipe came round again to the old chief, who scarcely allowed it to get cold before he had it filled again.

A PERILOUS JOURNEY.

In the year 1852, the Rev. R. Hunt undertook a journey to examine a spot supposed to be suitable for a missionary station. It was on the borders of a lake into which the river Saskatchewan was said to run; and this lake was reported to abound in fish. The name of this river signifies "the strong current;" but he hardly seems to have taken this hint of difficulty. A guide, a fisherman, and two Indian boys accompanied him; and they stepped into their canoe on the 12th of June, hoping to reach the lake on the second day. "About noon on the 13th," wrote Mr. Hunt, "we all deemed that we must reach the lake that night. We thought we heard the cry of lake-birds, and perceived other signs of its proximity; hence, as our provisions were getting low, I proposed to the fisherman that he and I should leave the canoe to be taken forward by the guide and the two Indian lads, while he and I should take a more direct course to the lake, so as to get the net into the water that night, in order to secure a breakfast of fish for the next morning. But it was thought better that the elder lad should accompany McLeod, the fisherman; and I took his place in the canoe. They soon found the path, as they supposed, and quickly disappeared from our sight. We then applied all our strength to urge forward the canoe; but the river had so many windings that we made but little progress, and about eleven at night, when it was too dark to ascertain our position, we were suddenly stopped by two large trees which had fallen into the river. As soon as the earliest light appeared, we renewed our efforts, and got past this hindrance. Our view was frequently intercepted by hills and tall pine-trees.

"Hour after hour we toiled expecting and hoping at every turn of the river to see the lake open upon us. The sun arose; noon came; the sun set; night came; but there seemed no termination of our toil; no appearance of the wished-for object. The two who had left us had no provisions. We ourselves had but one day's supply, and all our shot was gone. A little powder and one ball was all that remained; and these were reserved as a defence against the bears, which, we were told, were 'very wicked' hereabouts. I became anxious about McLeod and his companion, for had they discovered the lake, they might get tired of waiting for us and return by the path; and thus we might never meet. It was now eight days since we had left Fort

Nippewin, the nearest place we knew of at which we could find provisions. We knew that our two lost companions could never reach it without the canoe; nor did we see how any of us could reach it without provisions. Hunger and toil now forced us to rest for two or three hours. Early in the morning we renewed our efforts." About three, something which looked like a signal was seen, and they climbed a hill to the spot, but found only a pile of whitened bones. The two Indians climbed a tree; but not a sign of their companions was visible. Mr. Hunt then gave himself to prayer, and was about to write something which should indicate their fate in case they never returned, when this text caught his eye in Job xxiv. 5, "The wilderness yieldeth food for them and for their children." It revived his courage; and with his companions he again bent his knee and prayed that God would keep their feet, and in that time of necessity stretch out his hand to deliver them. Afterwards, he says, "we arose, and renewed our search for a path. In doing so we reached another part of the hill, whence a great prospect presented itself. I fancied that the wind brought me something like the sound of distant voices. I called in the aid of the practised eyes of the two young Indians, who soon detected in the plain before us two moving specks, which they declared to be human beings. Overjoyed, I immediately fired off two charges of powder, and raised and waved a white handkerchief. It caught their eyes; and we soon perceived them advancing towards us. In another quarter of an hour the keen eyes of the Indians assured us that these were our lost companions; and that God had indeed, and speedily, answered our prayers. We again fell on our knees and poured forth our thanks. All doubt and fear were now at an end; and we prepared to welcome our lost ones with as plentiful a meal as our scanty store could give. They had found no lake, but had been bewildered like ourselves, justly fearing that they should die except they found us. Glad and thankful were we once more to turn our boat's head down the stream. Soon she danced merrily on the waves of the 'strong current;' and we spared not to paddle stoutly night and day. On the third day we killed a large rat, and soon afterwards a goose; and shortly after this we fell in with some Indians, from whom we obtained a supply of food, which sufficed to carry us to our home."

ROUGH TRAVELLING.

Some years ago Mr. Watkins proceeded from Fort George to visit a post two hundred and forty miles northward, where he hoped to meet a considerable number of the Esquimaux. He was accompanied by Peter, a converted Esquimaux, and a party of his people; and two sleds, drawn by seven dogs, carried the missionary and.his provisions. This journey occupied sixteen days, amidst extreme cold, piercing winds, and horrid drifts of snow. At the termination of the first day's journey, the Esquimaux soon housed themselves in igloes, or snow-houses. Our missionary had brought with him an Indian deer-skin tent; but to pitch this was no easy matter. The snow lay four feet deep. First of all, therefore, they had to clear a circular space ten or eleven feet in diameter. To this work Mr. Watkins, assisted by one of the Esquimaux women, addressed himself, using his snow-shoe as a shovel; but his feet being thus deprived of the broad support it gave him, he sank knee-deep in the snow, and in that awkward position was obliged to work. Meanwhile, Peter was cutting down slender pines for tent-poles, and another person brought brushwood, which, when the hole in the snow was complete, was spread on the floor to serve as a bed, and piled up against the circular wall of snow around, to prevent its being melted by the heat of the fire. The tent-poles were then placed round the edge of the excavation, their upper ends coming to a point over the centre. On this framework the tent was spread, then dry wood procured, a fire kindled, the blankets spread, cooking utensils and provisions brought from the sled, and our missionary's house was complete. But it proved by no means comfortable; the smoke caused many tears, and the body of the inmate was too warm on one side, and nearly as cold as the surrounding snow on the other. He dispensed with the tent next night, and took up his abode in the snow-house.

CANOE TRAVELLING.

Mr. Hunt says: "By far the pleasantest rapids to run are, in my opinion, like a succession of such deep streams as passed through the most dangerous arch of old London Bridge, when the tide was fast flowing or ebbing; the more exciting those that dash and foam among large masses of rocks and stones. They are, generally, commenced by a gradual gliding together and sinking of the waters. At these parts, if an Indian is not very well acquainted with the place, he stands upright at the head of the canoe, taking care to tread exactly in the middle, and to balance himself perfectly; any attempt to change places in these canoes is to exchange the canoe for the water. In this position he sends a hasty glance down the rapid, and then, with voice and hand, he gives general directions as to the course to be taken; after which, down he sits in the bottom of the canoe, not crouching for fear, but in a really noble attitude; no longer like a stuffed boa, but with energy leaping out at every muscle. Every moment even life may depend upon a glance of his eye, or one turn of his paddle; he weighs opposite dangers, and decides with prompt and unerring judgment. Down, down, we go; his eye appears to be everywhere, and the canoe itself seems to possess the spirit of the Indians at the head and stern; for where they perceive she ought to be, there she is immediately, her own impetus wanting only their guiding will. They also see invisible things shadowed in the motions of the water, and thus avoid many a sunken stone. Sometimes not a voice can be heard for the dash of the water; and directions are given by the Indian forward by the motions of the head and hand. Thus we have run many a rapid of half a mile or more in fewer minutes

Arrival of Canoes at an Up-country Station in Rupert's Land. p. 218.

than it took us hours to ascend it. Whoever thinks these people irreclaimable savages, has surely never seen them run a first-rate rapid; a sight that would draw all London to it, if it could be transported to the Thames."

THE ARRIVAL AND DEPARTURE OF CANOES.

The short summer of Hudson's Bay is indeed a busy time, and a great deal has to be accomplished while it lasts. Down to the various forts come the canoes laden with furs collected during the winter season; and no sooner are they unladen than they are filled again with all the provisions that can be carried back for the coming year. Bales of blankets, bags of flour, chests of tea, cases of guns,—all are piled in rapidly; for they must be back before the frost sets in, or they will not arrive at their destination at all. The week that the Indians remain thus occupied is a busy one for the missionaries; for during every resting moment they are at the encampment. When all are ready to start, nearly all the inhabitants of the fort assemble to see them off; there is a general shaking of hands, and then up goes the flag; a parting salute, and the canoes are off.

A BLESSING FOUND IN THE BACKWOODS.

Mr. Kirkby, who has charge of the Mackenzie River District, one of the most northerly of all those in Rupert's Land, reports the happy death of a Christian friend, a tradesman in the employ of the Hudson's Bay Company. His conversion was as interesting as remarkable. He came from England a careless, thoughtless man. From York Factory he was sent up to Norway House in a boat manned by Christian Indians. During the voyage of twenty days, the example of these poor Indians was blessed by God to his highest good. He noticed their habit of morning and evening prayer, their kindness to himself, and their devout observance of the Lord's day. Other boats might go on, but not theirs. He was distressed to think that he, who had just come from a land of Christian privileges, should be so careless of his soul, and forgetful of his Saviour, whilst these red Indians cared for the one and loved the other. One evening, whilst the Indians were at their prayers, he plunged into the woods, and, falling on his knees, for the first time in his life, sought God's pardoning mercy. He found it. Now in heaven, we trust, he has testified to the fidelity of these Indians, who, wherever they went, "preached the gospel."

TESTIMONY OF INDEPENDENT WITNESSES.

In October of 1857, some Canadian gentlemen sent out by the Government on an exploratory expedition, but unconnected with missionary work, visited the Indian settlement under Mr. Cowley's care. The following, written by one of them, is an account of what they saw:—

"The church at the Indian settlement is a new and spacious building of stone, with a wall of the same material enclosing the churchyard, in which is a wooden schoolhouse, where I saw about fifty Ojibway Indians,—young men, young women, and children,—receiving instruction from the Rev. A. Cowley, Mrs. Cowley, and a native schoolmaster. The young Indian women read the New Testament in soft, low voices, but with ease and intelligence. During service the church was about three-fourths full. The congregation appeared to be exclusively Indian; in behaviour they were most decorous and attentive. The singing was very sweet, and all the forms of the service appeared to be understood and practised quietly, and in order, by the dusky worshippers. A seraphine was played by Mrs. Cowley to accompany the singers. The responses were well and exactly made, and the utmost attention was given to the sermon. The prayers were read in English, the lessons in Ojibway, and the sermon was delivered in Cree. After service, an Indian child, neatly dressed in white, was baptized. A few of the women and girls wore bonnets, but the greater number drew their shawls over their heads. A wonderful contrast do the subdued Indian worshippers in this missionary village present on a Sunday to the heathen revellers of the prairies, who perform their disgusting ceremonies within a mile and a half from some of the Christian churches of Red River. The farm attached to the Indian mission is cultivated with more than ordinary care: wheat, barley, Indian corn, and potatoes are the chief crops. The potato crop is here truly magnificent. . . . In the garden I noticed asparagus growing luxuriantly, beet, cabbages, brocoli, shallots, and, indeed, most culinary vegetables. In the farm-yard were ducks, fowls, turkeys, pigs, sheep, with some excellent milking cows. In the garden around the house some flowering-shrubs and annuals were still in bloom on the 3d of October. The air was fragrant with the perfume of mignonette, and the bright orange-yellow escholtzia shone pre-eminent among asters and sweet peas, which had escaped the autumn frosts."

COMMENCEMENT OF THE MORAVIAN MISSION IN THE WEST INDIES.

While a settlement of the Moravian and Bohemian exiles was forming at Herrnhut, a strong missionary spirit was awakened in this community of believers, and an especial interest was felt for the negroes. An opportunity soon presented itself to labour among them.

It was at the coronation of Christian VI., King of Denmark, that some of the brethren in the retinue of Count Zinzendorf met with a West Indian negro, and learned from him that often, while a slave on the Danish Island of St. Thomas, he had longed and sighed for a knowledge of the gospel, of which he had got some notion from the remarks made by white people. It was at Copenhagen, where he came with his master, that he had first heard the "glad tidings which are to all people;" and with joy he believed, and was baptized by the name of Anthony.

He spoke in a tone of strong feeling of the miserable state of the slaves of St. Thomas, and dwelt particularly on the condition of his own sister, who, like himself, desired to become acquainted with God; and while he spoke, the hearts of two of his hearers, Leonard Dober and Tobias Leupold, burned within them to go forth and be the messengers of salvation to Anthony's sister. These young men were intimate friends; but it was not until they had spent a night in prayer and tears that each discovered that the other had the same desire. Soon after, in speaking of the same subject, Anthony added that he thought it would be scarcely possible for a European to teach the blacks unless he submitted to slavery himself. But this made no difference in their wishes. They offered themselves to the congregation; and, after some time, the difficulties which stood in Leonard Dober's way were removed. For the present Leupold was compelled to remain at home. David Nitschman was then chosen as Dober's companion; and with the general direction from the brethren to follow the guidance of the Spirit of Christ in all things, they set forth on their journey to Copenhagen, a distance of six hundred miles. They had each about one pound of their own, and to this the count had added a present of a ducat each, that is, about nine shillings. At Copenhagen they were regarded as fools, and positively refused a passage in any Danish vessel; but at length, through Councillor Pless, the queen and Princess Amelia heard of and desired to see them; and on them their simple story had such an effect, that they were dismissed with most gracious promises of protection; and soon after the princess sent them a present of a sum of money and a large Dutch Bible. The negroes spoke a sort of Dutch dialect; so this was particularly acceptable. At last, also, they obtained a passage in a Dutch vessel; and during the interval of waiting they gained several friends, who, besides paying their passage-money, gave them the means of procuring tools for their respective trades: Dober was a potter, and his companion a carpenter. Immediately after landing at St. Thomas's, they went in search of Anthony's sister; and after delivering her brother's message, they preached to her and to her husband, and to the other blacks who gathered round them from the woods, "And this is life eternal, that they might know Thee, the only true God, and Jesus Christ whom thou has sent." The message was joyfully received, and ere long several, among whom were Anthony's sister and her husband, gave evidence that the word of God was taking root in their hearts. After five months, Leonard Dober was left alone; for his friend had only agreed to be his journey companion; and he had to return to his family. Nevertheless, the solitary labourer's way was made clear for him. Instead of being obliged to become a slave, the governor engaged him as tutor to his little children, and took him into his house, giving him leave to teach the negroes whenever he could get access to them. And he laboured on patiently alone, until, in about a year and a half, he was suprised by the arrival of a large party of the brethren, who had come out to work with him in these islands. We cannot follow them through their various difficulties and trials for want of space. It must suffice to say that when Count Zinzendorf visited these missions in 1738, just five years and a half after Dober's arrival, he was astonished to find eight hundred people who regularly attended the preaching of the gospel. So abundantly had God blessed and honoured his faithful servants.

THE END.

INDEX.

www.ingramcontent.com/pod-product-compliance
Lightning Source LLC
LaVergne TN
LVHW010250110826
845151LV00004B/1437

* 9 7 8 1 4 2 5 5 2 3 4 8 0 *